In 1994, Odeneho Nana Oduro Numapau II,
President of the Ghana National House of Chiefs,
initiated ceremonies in Africa and the Americas
to beg forgiveness of African Americans
for his ancestors' involvement in the slave trade.
In recognition of this extraordinary event,
this book is dedicated
to him.

African Kingdoms of the Past

Kongo
Ndongo

West
Central
Africa

Kenny Mann

Dillon Press • Parsippany, New Jersey

ACKNOWLEDGMENTS

The author wishes to acknowledge the interest, patience, and expertise of the following consultants: Clarence G. Seckel, Jr., Curriculum Coordinator of Social Studies, School District 189, East Saint Louis, IL; Edna J. Whitfield, Social Studies Supervisor (retired), St. Louis Public Schools, St. Louis, MO; and Dr. John K. Thornton, Associate Professor of History, Millersville University, Millersville, PA.

CREDITS

Design and Illustration: Maryann Zanconato
Picture Research: Kenny Mann and Valerie Vogel

PHOTO CREDITS

All photographs by Silver Burdett Ginn (SBG) unless otherwise noted.
Front Cover: © Hughes Dubois Photographie, Brussels.
José Pessoa/Museu e Laboratorio Anthropologico Coimbra/Courtesy, Arquivo Nacional de Fotografia: 35. José Pessoa/Museu Nacional de Etnologia/Courtesy, Arquivo Nacional de Fotografia: 41, 67. © Hughes Dubois Photographie, Brussels: 69. E.T. Archive: 57. Mary Evans Picture Library: 17, 55, 62–63, 90–91. The Granger Collection, New York: 56. The Hutchison Library: 24, 24–25, 70, 94, 95, 96; © B. Gerard: Title page, 93. Instituto Português dos Museus Arquivo Nacional de Fotografia: 86. Museo Naval, Madrid: 58. Mirabella Ricciardi: 37. Private Collection. Photo by Peter Terrail: 53. Courtesy, John Thornton: 66. W. Schneider Schütz/Staatliche Museen Preußischer Kulturbesitz, Museum für Völkerkunde, Berlin: 87. Maps, Ortelius Design: 6, 23, 26.

Library of Congress Cataloging-in-Publication Data
Mann, Kenny.
     Kongo, Ndongo: West Central Africa / Kenny Mann. — 1st ed.
     p. cm. — (African kingdoms of the past)
     Includes bibliographical references and index.
     ISBN 0-87518-658-0 (LSB). — ISBN 0-382-39298-1 (pbk.)
  1. Kongo (African people)—History—Juvenile literature. 2. Kongo (African people)—Folklore—Juvenile literature.
3. Ndongo (African people)—History—Juvenile literature. 4. Ndongo (African people)—Folklore—Juvenile literature.
5. Oral tradition—Angola—Juvenile literature. 6. Slave-trade—Angola—History—Juvenile literature. 7. Portugal—Colonies—Africa—Juvenile literature. 8. Angola—History—Juvenile literature. I Title. II. Series.
DT560.K66M35   1996   95-31307
966'.004963931—dc20

Summary: A survey of the oral traditions and history of the African kingdoms of Kongo and Ndongo, which once occupied the region of west central Africa that is now the nation of Angola. This study also offers insight into the kingdoms' relationship with Portugal and participation in the slave trade.

Published by Dillon Press,
A Division of Simon & Schuster,
299 Jefferson Road, Parsippany, New Jersey 07054

First edition
Printed in the United States of America
10 9 8 7 6 5 4 3 2 1

Table of Contents

African Kingdoms

Note: Dates marked with an * are approximate.

50,000	**B.C.**	**A.D. 500**	**1200**	**1400**

*50,000 B.C.	Early peoples living in what is now Angola
*2000 B.C.	Western Stream of Bantu people settles in central Africa
*500 B.C.	Bantu settle in northern Angola
*350 B.C.	Bantu learn to make iron tools and weapons
*300 B.C.	Mayan calendar invented
214 B.C.	Great Wall of China built

A.D. 200	Kingdom of Ghana established in western Sudan
711	North African Muslims (Moors) conquer Spain
1143	Portugal becomes independent from Spain
1180s	Kingdom of Kongo founded
1270	Eighth and last Crusade sets out; Aztecs are at height of power
1419	Prince Henry the Navigator begins financing expeditions down African coast
1434	Portuguese captain Gil Eames rounds Cape Bojador
1442	First West African slaves taken to Lisbon
1450s	Age of exploration begins
1453	Turks capture Constantinople; seek new routes to the East

1483	Diogo Cão arrives at mouth of Zaire River, takes four African hostages to Europe
1485	Cão returns to Kongo with hostages
1491	Portuguese fleet arrives at mouth of the Zaire; *mwene Soyo* and *mwene Kongo* baptized
1492	Christopher Columbus arrives in the Americas
1498	Vasco da Gama rounds the Cape of Good Hope on his way to India
1506	Dom Afonso I crowned king of Kongo
1520s	São Tomé becomes one of the world's leading sugar producers
1526	Afonso writes to king of Portugal complaining about slave trade
1543	King Afonso I dies
1550s	Ndongo founded
1568	Imbangala invade Kongo
1591	Filippo Pigafetta writes an account of the Kingdom of Kongo

	1600		**1700**		**2000**

1600	Slavery introduced to Americas
1622	Njinga of Ndongo signs peace treaty with Portuguese governor Correia de Souza
1624–	Njinga fights Ngola Hari and
1655	Portuguese over succession to Ndongo throne
1630s	Province of Soyo breaks away from kingdom of Kongo
1641	Dutch arrive in Luanda
1647–	Njinga and the Dutch join
1648	forces against the Portuguese
1648	Portuguese fleet from Brazil arrives in Luanda; Dutch surrender and depart
1656	Peace treaty with the Portuguese signed; boundaries of Mbundu kingdom defined
1656	Witchcraft trials held in Salem, Massachusetts
1658	Father Antonio Gaeta da Napoli records Njinga's life history

1663	Queen Njinga dies
1665	Battle of Mbwila; civil war breaks out in Kongo
1686	Beatriz Kimpa Vita born
1704	Beatriz Kimpa Vita possessed by Saint Anthony
1706	Beatriz Kimpa Vita burned at the stake
1776	American colonies declare independence from Great Britain
1791	Slaves from Kongo and Ndongo help to overthrow French government in Haiti

1920s	Portuguese immigrants settle in Angola
1955	King Pedro VII, last king of Kongo, dies
1956	Popular Movement for the Liberation of Angola (MPLA) formed
1961	Front for the Liberation of Angola (FNLA) formed
1965	National Union for the Total Independence of Angola (UNITA) formed; rival rebel groups battle for power
1975	Portugal withdraws from Angola
1992	Election held in Angola; MPLA wins, but rival factions continue fighting
1994	Angolans sign truce

Introduction

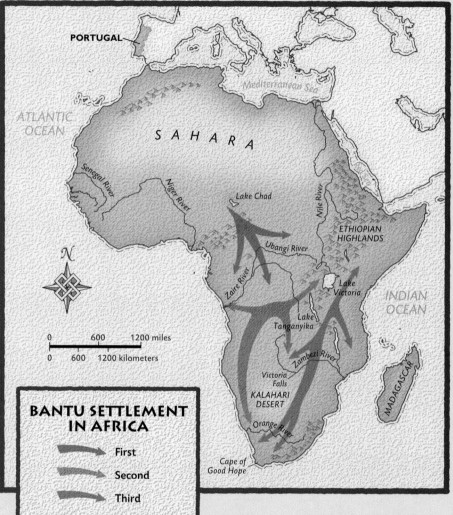

Between 500 B.C. and A.D. 1500, the Bantu migrated from Central Cameroon, a region south of the Sahara, to the central, western, eastern, and southern regions of the continent.

Map labels: PORTUGAL, Mediterranean Sea, ATLANTIC OCEAN, SAHARA, Senegal River, Niger River, Lake Chad, Nile River, ETHIOPIAN HIGHLANDS, Ubangi River, Zaire River, Lake Victoria, INDIAN OCEAN, Lake Tanganyika, Zambezi River, MADAGASCAR, Victoria Falls, KALAHARI DESERT, Orange River, Cape of Good Hope

N

0   600   1200 miles
0   600   1200 kilometers

BANTU SETTLEMENT IN AFRICA

First
Second
Third

For nearly 500 years, from the late fifteenth century to the late twentieth century, the region of west central Africa now called Angola had close and mostly unhappy relations with the European nation of Portugal. During its time as a Portuguese colony, Angola was torn by war and conquest, and its people lived in poverty and experienced much suffering.

Before the colonial period, however, despite much local warfare, the region had been divided into flourishing kingdoms. People there raised crops and tended animals. They lived out their lives within the framework of a belief system that helped them to respect and understand their environment. Their kings and queens ruled with an iron hand. There was little other than the kingdoms' own internal stresses and strains to disturb them.

Who were these people? Where did they come from? How were they able to thrive in an environment that was deadly to most of the early Europeans who tried to live there?

There are clues to these questions all over Angola. Evidence of human habitation in the region thousands of years ago has been found in many places. Marks on rocks, massive stone pillars, and prehistoric tools are just a few of the signs that people have lived in Angola since about 50,000 B.C., perhaps even much earlier.

The visible signs tell one story. The invisible signs revealed by carbon dating and other modern techniques tell another. A link between the visible and the invisible has been provided by the study of language.

Languages change as groups of people move from one area to another, adapt to their surroundings, and intermarry with other groups. By observing language changes over time and distance, historians can track the movements of related groups of people from one location to another.

Scholars of African history have divided the African people into various language groups. One of these is the Bantu group. The word *ntu* (N too)*, common to over 400 languages in this language family, means "person." *Ba-ntu* is simply the plural form, meaning "people."

The oral traditions of the Bantu people generally place them in their current locations only about 500 years ago. But modern historians have learned that the Bantu were already on the move and had reached their present locations much earlier. The original Bantu language seems to have evolved in the region of present-day Cameroon. From there, it spread eastward and southward

The word for "bird" in Kiswaheli, which is spoken all over eastern Africa, is *ndege* (n-DE-ge). In Angola, however, the word is *ndele* (n-DE-le). The two words have the same Bantu root, but have altered slightly over time and in different regions.

* Words that may be difficult to pronounce have been spelled phonetically in parentheses. A pronunciation key appears on page 98.

The origin of the name *Kongo* is lost in time. In the Kikongo language, *ku-ngo* (kuh-n-goh) means "the land of the leopard." The word for "hunter" is *nkongo*, while that for a "hurled weapon" is *kongo* or *kong*. The word *kongo* also refers to a powerful, high-born individual—someone likely to become a king or noble. The name for the kingdom could have arisen from any or all of these sources, especially since all these words refer to symbols of power.

as the Bantu spread out over the continent. The Bantu did not migrate in large numbers, as was originally thought. Rather, small traveling groups gradually infiltrated new areas and intermarried with the hunter-gatherers and farmers native to those places.

By about 2000 B.C., Bantu of the so-called Western Stream had settled in the deep forests of central Africa. Here, they learned to plant yams and other root crops and to tend the trees that bore fruit, oil, palm nuts, bark, and other useful products. They kept goats and cleared the forest with simple stone axes.

The stone tools of these early Bantu people limited their hunting and farming techniques. Imagine the labor required to cut down a giant tree with only stone axes! It was easier for these early peoples to cultivate land and hunt in the open savannah, which they found beyond the Zaire (zeye EER) River, in what is now northern Angola. They settled there around 500 B.C. By 350 B.C., these Bantu had learned how to make tools and weapons out of iron.

It is not clear whether knowledge of ironworking was carried south to Angola from the ancient Nile City of Meroë (ME roh), which flourished as an iron-making center, or whether it came from East Africa, where people were smelting iron ore as early as the seventh century B.C. It could be that the early Bantu actually discovered the technique themselves. No one knows for certain, but ironworking definitely lifted the Bantu out of the Stone Age. Now they could make tools and weapons that were sharper, more practical, and more durable than those made of stone, bone, or wood. They became better hunters, better farmers, and better warriors, truly adapted to life in their newfound environments.

Once the Western Stream Bantu had settled in the region, they were able to develop the rich culture and political system that have fascinated historians ever since the first Portuguese arrived at the mouth of the Zaire River in 1483. The great kingdom of Kongo (not to be confused with the modern nation of Congo) had been founded in what is now northern Angola some 300 years earlier, when Europe still floundered in the Dark Ages.

In the early years after the arrival of the Portuguese, the Kongo kings welcomed the newcomers as profitable new trading partners. The kings wanted the benefits of European technology and the skills of reading and writing. The Portuguese, for their part, had come as traders, not conquerors, and naturally hoped for profitable business relations. They had also come with the fervent desire to introduce Christianity to Africa, and were amazed when the Kongo nobility seemed more than willing to embrace the Catholic faith.

Having developed in different places thousands of miles apart, the two cultures were very different from each other. Yet they were also similar in some respects.

Portugal had separated from Spain and established itself as an independent kingdom in the mid-twelfth century, just as Kongo was on the rise. Around the same time, the Portuguese expelled the Moors, who had invaded the region from North Africa several centuries earlier. The Moorish influence in Portuguese life and culture remained strong, however, and after several centuries of intermarriage with the Moors, the Portuguese had developed "brotherly" attitudes toward other dark-skinned peoples. In Angola and other African territories, they easily intermarried with Africans and absorbed some of their culture.

Portugal was divided into two very distinct classes: the peasant class and the ruling class. The peasants had little to do with the ruling class and cared little for the nobility's ideas of expansion and empire. They preferred to continue their traditional occupations of farming, small trading, and shopkeeping.

Kongo society was similarly divided. Legends recall that the ruling class were "strangers" who had come from "the north" to conquer the local people. The ruling class lived in the towns, and the peasants occupied small villages. The ruling class also had grand ideas of expanding the kingdom. Once the Portuguese arrived, the ruling class became deeply involved in international trade, while the peasants merely provided trade goods—especially the raffia cloth for which Kongo became famous.

Anthropologists have recently coined the term *Bakongo* to describe speakers of the Kikongo language. Kikongo-speakers inhabit a region much larger than the original kingdom of Kongo. The inhabitants of the kingdom itself called themselves *Esikongo*, or "citizens of the kingdom of Kongo." No other people, although they spoke the same language, would have used the term *Esikongo*.

Both nations were also intensely nationalistic, although in different ways. The Portuguese were determined that their tiny country be recognized as a mighty world power. Threatened by the superior power of Spain, Portugal had developed something of an inferiority complex. It had no choice but to look outward, beyond its own borders. By the early fifteenth century, the Portuguese had begun their brief period of glory. For a hundred years, they were the world leaders in navigation, exploration, conquest, and trade on three continents.

The Kongo leaders also wanted their kingdom to be the greatest and most powerful in the region. Unlike the Portuguese, though, they were not threatened by a superior power. Indeed, many European visitors noted that the Esikongo—the inhabitants of the kingdom—believed themselves to be the best, the happiest, and the most fortunate people on earth! It had

Kongo Men

Many Europeans were impressed by the Esikongo. These illustrations of Esikongo men and women were probably drawn by an artist who had read a report written by Duarte Lopes, a Portuguese sailor who visited Kongo in 1578. ▶

never entered their heads that the day might come when they too might be conquered.

Trade, Christianity, and peaceful brotherhood were the hallmarks of the new relationship between the Kongo nation and Portugal. During the first years of the Kongo-Portuguese alliance, it seemed that the cooperative experiment between the two nations might actually succeed. Sadly, this was not to be. Christianity was soon absorbed into age-old Kongo beliefs. The climate and tropical diseases proved deadly to the Portuguese. The peaceful trade of cloth, ivory, and other local goods soon gave way to the abominations of the slave trade. And civil war finally brought about the kingdom's downfall. The great experiment failed.

What had happened in the kingdom of Kongo influenced the state of Ndongo (DON goh), farther south. Some Kongo kings claimed that Ndongo was a vassal state under Kongo's control. In fact, Kongo and Ndongo had always been rivals, but Ndongo was unable to establish itself as a kingdom until the late sixteenth century, when it profited handsomely from the slave trade.

Both Kongo and Ndongo were eventually absorbed into the Portuguese colony of Angola. How might these kingdoms have developed without European intervention? Would they have continued in the age-old ways? Or would other factors have led to their downfall? These are questions that occupy historians of the region.

Kongo Women

"The climate here [in Kongo] is so unhealthy for the foreigner that of all those who go there, few fail to sicken, and of those who sicken, few fail to die, and those who survive are obliged to withstand the intense heat of the torrid zone, suffering hunger, thirst, and many other miseries for which there is no relief save patience, of which much is needed . . . to tolerate the discomforts of such a wretched place."
— A sixteenth-century report

KONGO

Kongo—The Founding Stories

Nimi A Lukeni:
Crossing the Zaire River

A long, long time ago, in the province of Corimba, near the great Zaire River, there lived a woman named Ne Lukeni (ne loo KAY nee) [Lady Lukeni]. She was married, and, in time, she bore her husband a son, named Nimi a Lukeni (Nimi, son of Lukeni). The boy grew to be a strong, healthy youth, defiant in nature and eager for power.

One day, Ne Lukeni wished to cross the great river to reach a market on the other side. The ferryman there kept her waiting, and Ne Lukeni became impatient. She berated the man and badgered him endlessly. She was pregnant, she shouted. She should cross immediately!

It did not pay to annoy the ferryman. After all, he was master of these waters, and no one could cross the great river without his services.

"Perhaps you are a queen," he sneered, "or at least the mother of a king, that you cannot wait patiently like everyone else. When the other passengers have crossed, then you, too, may cross the river."

Ne Lukeni was furious. How dare this lowly ferryman treat her so insolently!

KONGO

Ne Lukeni returned home and told her son, Nimi a Lukeni, what had happened. Now the young man saw at once his chance to seize the power for which he yearned.

"Console yourself, Mother," her son said, "for this I promise you. You shall indeed be the mother of a king. And I, Nimi a Lukeni, shall be that king. But first, I must have a kingdom."

From then on, Nimi a Lukeni had only one aim. He would cross the Zaire and conquer the rich and fertile lands to the south of the great river.

Nimi a Lukeni recruited many people, luring them with promises of land and great riches. In time, he departed from his homeland with all his followers, his father, mother, and sister, and set out to make his promise come true.

With the cunning of a jackal, Nimi a Lukeni entrenched himself in an area of impregnable mountain crags. This spot lay near the ancient trade routes reaching from the sea coast deep into the interior, and from the north to the south. Many people traveled these paths, carrying with them salt and valuable shell money, cloth, ivory, foodstuffs, and other precious items of trade. From his rocky fortress, Nimi a Lukeni and his armed followers were able to ambush the travelers. They took their goods and forced them to pay heavy tolls in order to pass.

Nimi a Lukeni also conducted fierce raids into the land surrounding his outpost. He found criminals, outcasts, adventurers, and men of greed to join his forces. Before long, he had become known as a single-minded and unyielding leader, and his followers proclaimed him their king. From then on, he was addressed as *mwene* (MWE ne) *Kongo*—king of Kongo.

When he judged the time to be right, King Nimi invaded the lands across the Zaire. He fought and conquered as he marched, driving local lords from their ancestral lands. At length, King Nimi and his people reached a mountain known as Vumba. It was here that, with great foresight, the *mwene Kongo* chose to build his capital city.

At the top of the mountain, King Nimi found a wide, flat plain, in the center of which was a lake. He commanded his people to fill in the lake with earth. When this was done, they built houses and roads, and for their king, a palace.

The city came to be known as Mbanza (m BAHN zah) [city] Kongo. The site was truly chosen with great wisdom. It lay near the crossroads of trade, and for miles in all directions one could look far out over the land. The earth was rich and fertile. The sun shone, the rain fell, and the people prospered.

After his military triumphs, King Nimi proved to be a prudent and wise king. He laid down the first laws, which were just and true. In time, through strength and valor, he conquered other areas, and his capital was eventually surrounded by a vast territory consisting of many provinces.

One day, King Nimi assembled at his palace enclosure those relatives, companions, and slaves whom he deemed worthy. The *mwene Kongo* entered his dwelling and returned with the sacred knife that symbolized his dignity, his royalty, and his laws. Then he took also a buffalo tail, the other symbol of his royalty, and his people knelt before him. King Nimi raised his right hand, and all were silent.

King Nimi was indeed a wise man. To each of his selected people, he entrusted the governorship of a province. Each was to go forth for a period of not less than three years, governing wisely and bringing prosperity to his province, and thus to the kingdom.

"For two reasons the earliest lords of the country placed this territory on the said summit; first, because it lies in almost the very middle of the kingdom, whence subsidies could be quickly sent to every part; and then, because the natural elevation gives good air, a secure position, and one not to be taken by force.... There is no lack of water springs on this high plain ... to which the people descend ... and carry the water into the city in vessels of wood and terra cotta, and also in gourds on the shoulders of slaves."
—*Filippo Pigafetta, a description of Mbanza Kongo from* A Report of the Kingdom of Kongo, *1591*

In this way was the kingdom of Kongo formed, and it became the largest and most powerful of those lands along the western coast of central Africa. And in this way did Nimi a Lukeni keep his promise to his mother, Ne Lukeni, who did indeed become the mother of a king.

Truth and Myth

The story of Nimi a Lukeni has been handed down among the people of Kongo—the Esikongo—for many centuries. There are also other founding stories, quite different from the one told here. Which one is true? The answer varies, depending on who is telling the story and when.

The earliest known story, recorded in the 1580s, describes how several provinces simply joined together to form a kingdom, with one strong leader as king.

Later stories that resemble the one in this book were traditional during the seventeenth and early eighteenth centuries. They describe how Nimi a Lukeni conquered various provinces to become an all-powerful king. In one version, Nimi a Lukeni is the ferryman, wielding his power at the river crossing. In this story, the pregnant woman who wished to cross the river was his aunt, not his mother. It is said that Nimi a Lukeni killed her. Instead of treating him as a criminal, the people admired his hard-heartedness and proclaimed him their king, or *mwene Kongo*. He elected individuals — usually members of the royal family—as governors of the provinces and, relying on their loyalty, thus forged a new kingdom. This story of Nimi a Lukeni reflects the existing political structure at the time, since during the seventeenth and eighteenth centuries, the kings did in fact have absolute power.

After 1700 the stories claim that the founding king was a blacksmith, the inventor of the art of the forge. He provided his people with the iron tools of agriculture and the weapons of war. These were far superior to the implements of bone, wood, stone, and copper used by neighboring peoples. The blacksmith's people were thus able to produce more food and win more battles than their rivals. He naturally became a leader, and metalwork became the privilege of the Kongo nobility.

In Esikongo tradition, a blacksmith is a fair and just man. In these stories the king attained his power through his reputation for the wise and skillful judgment of disputes. Again, the blacksmith tradition is close to the real situation in Kongo during the eighteenth century. At that time, attempts were made to reduce the

In Kikongo the king was called the *mwene Kongo*. The Portuguese corrupted this to *mani Kongo*.

In Africa south of the Sahara, this short-handled hoe with an iron blade replaced the digging stick after the introduction of iron.

king's authority and redistribute power more equitably among the various provinces of the kingdom.

After 1850 the story changes yet again! At this time, local clans were more powerful and important than before. Thus it was natural for each clan to claim in its version of the story that it had founded and organized the kingdom.

Interpreting the Stories

Since the first Portuguese landed on the shores of Kongo in 1483, the history of the area has been extensively studied and documented. European officials, traders, and missionaries left behind a wealth of material in the form of books, diaries, letters, official records, and dictionaries. Although their paintings and drawings often reflect European tasks and values, they remain useful sources of information on Kongo life. While the Esikongo had previously relied on oral histories, they very soon became literate in the Portuguese language, and later in the

Kikongo language. Since 1491, they too have produced thousands of letters, documents, and scholarly works recording and analyzing the history of their own country.

All these chroniclers agree that Nimi a Lukeni, or the "founding father," and his clan came from a place "north of the Zaire" sometime during the mid-fourteenth century. Until the eighteenth century, the Esikongo regarded this ruling class as "foreigners" or "strangers."

Was the first *mwene Kongo* really a blacksmith? It is certainly possible.

Historians guess that many blacksmiths were also traders, seeking new markets for the copper that was mined in the regions north of the Zaire River. Different groups or clans had to cooperate with one another to create safe trade routes and a uniform system of taxation. They probably chose one man—perhaps Nimi a Lukeni—to be their leader. To represent them all, he would have had to break with his own clan.

It is possible that this leader took his clan farther south, conquering as he went and creating a new trade route in the process. The place where this route crossed an older east-west route leading inland from the coast may have proved the ideal place for the capital city. It is also possible that a chiefdom already existed where the trade routes crossed. Its leader may have seized the opportunity for greater power and built a capital city around a convenient marketplace. Either way, the kingdom was expanded through trade, conquest, and careful marriages with neighboring peoples.

There is probably some truth in each version of the founding story. It is also possible that the different versions are meant as allegories. They may be interpreted symbolically, much like ancient Greek myths and tales, or like "Cinderella" and "Jack the Giant Killer."

For example, Nimi a Lukeni could represent a character who had to be a ruthless outcast to earn the power he sought. He had to break the bonds with his clan by "killing" his relative. This would explain why he was revered rather than despised for his actions. Later he is said to have been "prudent and wise." In other words, a great leader must be both brutal and loving, both ruthless and just.

The fine details of the founding story may never be discovered. It is clear, however, that the first *mwene Kongo* and his followers were highly skilled, resourceful people. They forged a huge kingdom that knitted the Esikongo people together for 300 years. That kingdom is gone, and while the Esikongo still inhabit their homelands, it may not be long before their stories, too, are gone.

◀ A blacksmith uses bellows to create enough heat to smelt iron ore so that it can be shaped using the hammer and anvil. This painting was done in the seventeenth century by the Italian missionary, Antonio Cavazzi, who faithfully recorded all that he saw.

The Kingdom Flourishes

When Portuguese merchants arrived off the coast of West Africa in the 1470s, they were astonished to find a series of highly civilized kingdoms—Mali, Benin, Calabar, and others. The magnificently dressed rulers of these kingdoms wielded godly power; their royal households boasted untold wealth in gold, ivory, and slaves; and some of their cities rivaled those of Europe in size and splendor.

When the Portuguese arrived in the kingdom of Kongo in 1483, they found a very different but equally dazzling civilization, described as "the most powerful and magnificent country in all Guinea." They were to remain deeply involved in the region for almost 500 years.

The Kongo Region

The kingdom of Kongo was never clearly defined by boundaries. Several kings claimed a region stretching far north of the Zaire River and east to the Kwango River. Perhaps a kingdom of this size once existed, but kings were in the habit of claiming more territory than they actually controlled. In the sixteenth century, the kingdom was probably roughly bound to the north by the Zaire River, to the west by the Atlantic Ocean, to the east by the Nkisi (n KEE see) River, about 970 km (600 mi) inland, and from there in a southwesterly line to the island of Luanda on the coast. Historians estimate the population then at about 350,000 people. Today the area corresponds to the northwestern section of Angola and the eastern wedge of Zaire.

How did the kingdom rise to power? What did Nimi a Lukeni, or the first *mwene Kongo*, find that enabled him to forge many small provinces into an empire of over 250,000 sq. km (100,000 sq. mi)? More than anything else, historians believe, Nimi a Lukeni was lucky! He found a region abundant in water and rich in plant, animal, and mineral resources. He found local people with a language similar to his own. They knew their environment

Before the sixteenth century, the kingdom of Kongo may have been much larger, stretching north beyond the Zaire River as well as much farther south. Kongo kings often claimed part of the kingdom of Ndongo, to the south, as their own. ▶

THE KINGDOMS OF
WEST CENTRAL AFRICA

- Land over 1000 m (3300 ft)
- Land between 500 - 1000 m (1640 - 3300 ft)
- Land below 500 m (1640 ft)
- Approximate boundaries of Kongo Kingdon
- Approximate boundaries of Ndongo Kingdom
- Approximate boundaries of Matamba Kingdom
- Boundaries of modern nations

24

This view looks
out from the
craggy heights of
the eastern
mountains over
the flatter
central zone. ▶

The landscape in
southern Angola,
near Luanda,
is dry and
unwelcoming. ▼

intimately and were superb agriculturists. As a conqueror, Nimi a Lukeni had moved into a prime area, ripe for expansion and growth. He was greatly helped by the natural ecology of the region.

South of the Zaire River, there are three distinct ecological regions: the coastal zone, the central zone, and the plateau zone. Each runs roughly parallel to the coast.

The plateau zone, draining from the hills of the central zone into the Kwango River, is arid and inhospitable. Great ridges, barren and stony, traverse the land from north to south and are dissected by wooded river valleys. These supported only a few inhabitants, who raised cereal crops like sorghum and millet. The valleys are surrounded by flat-topped mountains

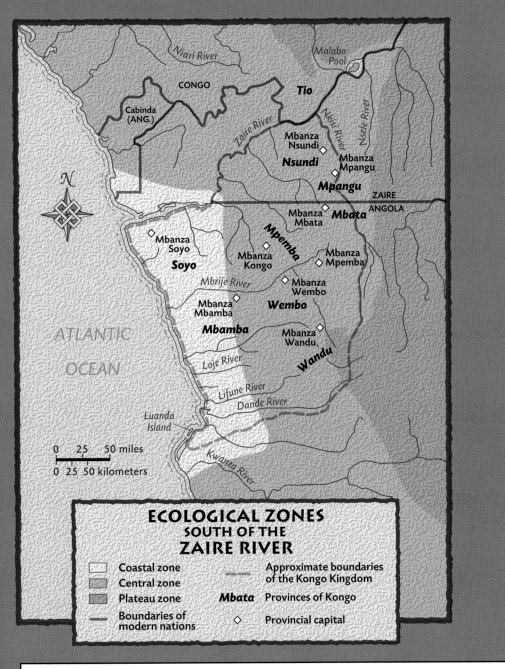

ECOLOGICAL ZONES SOUTH OF THE ZAIRE RIVER

- ☐ Coastal zone
- ☐ Central zone
- ☐ Plateau zone
- ━━━ Boundaries of modern nations
- ┅┅┅ Approximate boundaries of the Kongo Kingdom
- *Mbata* Provinces of Kongo
- ◇ Provincial capital

that look like fortresses and form natural barriers to invasion.

The backbone of the central zone is formed by a ridge of mountains, up to 1,200 m (3,600 ft) high, stretching south from the Zaire River. To the east they flatten out to form the plateau zone. To the west they drop gradually to the plains of the coastal zone.

Five hundred years ago, the vegetation ranged from savannah in the lower southwest to rain forest in the mountains, with intense cultivation in between. Because of its high rainfall and fertile soils, the central zone was, and still is, the most densely populated of the three.

▲ The central zone was always densely populated, as evidenced by the large number of provincial capitals located there. In the fifteenth and sixteenth centuries, there were eight major provinces in Kongo. Mbata and Mpangu, in the Nkisi River valley, produced raffia cloth. Nsundi, to the north, had access to the copper trade north of the Zaire River. Mbamba oversaw the collection of *nzimbu* shells from Luanda. Wembo controlled the copper mines farther east. Mpemba province was the location of the kingdom's capital, Mbanza Kongo. Soyo, to the west, was one of the strongest provinces. Its capital, Mbanza Soyo, later rivaled Mbanza Kongo in power and wealth. The southeastern province of Wandu eventually became the stronghold of Queen Njinga of Ndongo.

Nimi a Lukeni's capital city, Mbanza Kongo—later renamed São (sou) Salvador—stands in ruins today, 240 km (150 mi) east of the coast and 130 km (80 mi) south of the Zaire River. Located in the northern part of the central zone, it lies on a broad plateau, about 16 km (10 mi) in circumference and some 600 m (1,800 ft) above sea level. For about 32 km (20 mi) around the capital, the land was densely populated and heavily cultivated. Sixteenth-century observers estimated that the area supported between 60,000 and 100,000 inhabitants.

A great variety of crops and plants was cultivated in the central zone. Along the fertile valleys of the Nkisi River, for instance, at least eight types of palm flourished. The leaves of the raffia palm provided fibers that were woven into exquisite cloths of various sizes and quality that could be worn only by the king and his nobles. The Europeans compared them to the best and most costly silks, velvets, and taffetas. Their value was determined by their weight, place of origin, and weaving style, and they were frequently used as a form of currency.

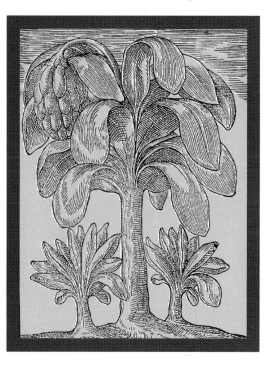

Other palms throughout the central zone provided palm oil, wine, vinegar, fruits, and bread, all derived from various parts of the tree. The Esikongo even made a salad dressing of the white milk that oozed out of a hole bored in the top of the tree. Palm tree leaves and trunks were used in buildings, game traps, fishing snares, clothing, cosmetics, and medicines.

The cola nut—fruit of the cola tree—was another major crop. It was used as a food, a thirst quencher, and a mild stimulant. The Esikongo also cultivated a wide variety of fruit unknown to Europeans. Later, their orchards produced guavas, lemons, and oranges, which were imported from Portugal.

The central zone was also rich in various grains, cultivated beans, peas, yams, bananas, and plantains. Imported peanuts, sugar cane, and pineapples also flourished. The Esikongo were also masters at collecting the "free" fruits of the wild—edible roots and tubers, leaves, berries, and over 20 species of mushrooms.

"It must be remembered that gold, silver and other metals . . . are not used as money in these countries. And so it happens that with gold and silver in abundance, either in mass or in coin, yet nothing can be bought except with shells."
— *Filippo Pigafetta, 1591*

▲ *Nzimbu* shells were used as currency.

The coastal zone, dropping down gradually from the high central plateau, was much less fertile. It suffered from low rainfall and loose, sandy soils. Most people lived along the Zaire estuary, where higher rainfall allowed the cultivation of rice in the muddy mangrove swamps. Near the southern coast, the sandy, acidic soils supported little more than grasses, thorn trees, and palms. Farther inland, the coast gave way to a rocky desert.

Along the beaches, women manufactured salt by boiling sea water. They also dove for special shells called *nzimbu* (n ZIHM boo), which were used as currency throughout the kingdom. The best shells were thin, shiny, and black and came from the island of Luanda, now part of the capital city of Angola. The men of the coastal zone produced a rough bark cloth by unrolling and pounding the bark of palm trees.

More than enough food was produced in all three zones for trade, although crops were sometimes devastated by drought, floods, swarms of locusts, or, in the central zone, elephants.

Wildlife was abundant everywhere. "Small game"—snakes, lizards, rats, and even insects and worms—was eaten. Larger game such as elephant, antelope, leopard, and buffalo was also consumed. Hunters had to go through elaborate rituals to protect themselves and honor the beasts they ate. Fish were also plentiful in the various rivers and lakes.

Rain fell in deluges from September to May. A Florentine priest traveling in the region in 1665 described walking for days in waist-high water, plagued by swarms of mosquitoes. Floods and mud slides were common. Crops and buildings were often ruined.

The dry season from May to September was a welcome respite. This was the time when people traded, visited relatives, enjoyed various social occasions, or went to war. Quite frequently, however, the dry season turned into disastrous drought. Crops failed, animals and people starved, and tensions ran high. Then people turned to the rainmaker, or *nganga* (n GAHN guh)—a person with magical powers. Understandably, the *nganga* played an extremely important role in Kongo society.

In this painting by Cavazzi, a seated nobleman examines raffia cloth displayed by a trader.

Men, Women, and Work

Labor was strictly divided between men and women. The women were fairly skilled potters. They worked the land, sowing, tending, and harvesting the many crops. They also did all the collecting of wild berries, roots, and other edible plants. Women cooked and took care of children and domestic animals and participated in many of the sacred Esikongo rituals.

The men cleared the forests and scrub. They harvested many tree crops, such as palm oil, palm wine, and fruit, and made medicines from plant and animal products. They built houses out of branches and thatch and also hunted, fished, and traded.

Some men were artisans, with the blacksmiths holding the highest positions. Knowledge of metalworking may have spread west from East Africa some time during the four-

teenth century—just when historians pinpoint the founding of the kingdom.

Iron ore was commonly found in the rocks of the Kongo region, and the blacksmiths were experts at their art. They also knew how to melt lead and to forge copper and tin. Recent evidence has shown that they were aware of lead poisoning and had an effective cure for it: massive doses of mashed papaya doused in palm oil.

Limited amounts of copper were found within the kingdom, but there were rich deposits north of the Zaire River. The copper deposits may have played a role in the formation of the kingdom, as explained in Chapter 1. Copper would continue to influence Kongo's history for several centuries.

Copper was used for ceremonial and religious objects. Men and women wore as many elaborate bracelets and armbands as possible. People were

A Kongo woman cultivates her field using an iron hoe, while another woman carries wares in her basket for sale at market. Behind the women stands a thatched granary. ▶

reported wearing up to 12 kg (25 lbs) of copper at one time! Perhaps this show was merely decorative, but it may have been meant to indicate wealth and status.

Woodworkers were highly revered and made figurines for ritual, magic, or protective use. They also made drums, which were played at celebrations and in times of war. In addition, woodworkers produced simple furniture and household items. Civet (a species of wildcat) and otter skins were reserved for the nobility. Expert basket makers used local wicker to make containers and fishing nets. And many European

visitors were amazed at the men's skill at weaving the famed raffia cloth and other textiles, which rivaled European textiles in their texture and beauty.

Cult, Status, and Society

The Esikongo saw a natural hierarchy, or ranking, in plant, animal, and human life. Thus the work that men and women did and the natural materials they used defined their positions in society. Men who wove the raffia cloth, for example, enjoyed a higher status than those who made the rougher bark cloth.

The Esikongo had a rich oral tradition. Their lives were enriched by poems, ritual songs and phrases, prayers, speeches, love songs, eulogies, praises, stories, proverbs, riddles, and other forms of verbal expression. To them, words were the source of good and evil. Words formed messages to the ancestors and gave individuals the power to act. Words praised the king at the magnificent ceremonies, and thus reinforced the greatness of the kingdom. The praises were intoned by heralds to a solemn accompaniment of lutes and drums.

Members of this secret society in Kongo were photographed in 1914. They covered their bodies with pipe clay and wore grass skirts held up by ceremonial belts. ▼

Blacksmiths were considered superior to woodworkers. A leopard skin was more "noble" than that of a civet. And the palm tree was the noblest tree of all.

Esikongo society had many other divisions. The *kitome* (kih TOH me) were individuals responsible for maintaining harmony between people and the natural world by praying to important ancestors and dieties. They were believed to bring or withhold rain. They blessed the seed, gave permission for the harvest, and received its first fruits. They were responsible for the fertility of people, plants, and animals. The *kitome* usually performed their rituals near sacred bodies of water, which were believed to form the boundary between this world and the next. The *kitome* beloned to a class of priests called *nganga*.

Several secret and powerful cults also ruled Esikongo society. The most influential of these was the *kimpasi* (kihm-PAH see). The *kimpasi* cult had to do with suffering. Members of this cult believed that they had "died" and were then reborn, their bodies possessed by an ancestor spirit. Another cult was connected with water and earth spirits. The *mwene Kongo* also headed a cult, which was concerned with the graves of former kings. Yet another cult centered around the powers of destruction and protection, as symbolized by whirlwinds and other forces of nature.

When the Portuguese arrived, bringing Christianity with them, the Esikongo leaders adopted the religion as another cult—one that would eventually influence the entire region.

The Tribute System

Mountains effectively separated the people of the three zones, so that they even spoke different dialects of their common language, Kikongo. In addition, each zone produced different commodities. The products of the coastal zone had low value there, but high value farther east. Similarly, products of the east were highly valued in the west.

This fact allowed the Esikongo to devise a clever system of enforced tribute and tax that linked the three zones economically and politically, making each dependent on the

> A cult can be defined as a system of religious belief and ritual.

KIKONGO WORDS

Esikongo	the people of Kongo
Mukongo	an individual
kanda	a social group sharing a common interest
kitome	a spiritual leader of a particular cult
mwene	Lord or king
nzimbu	shell money

other. This practice may have existed in regions north of the Zaire River and as far south as Luanda long before the kingdom was founded.

Key to the system were powerful groups of people known as *kanda*. A *kanda* could be any social group that shared a common interest, and each

town, village, and province usually had several *kanda*. The *kanda* organized markets in different locations at different times during the four-day Kongo week. They were probably also responsible for collecting taxes and tribute and passing them on to the king.

Historians believe that the earliest *kanda* were absorbed into Kongo. Their leaders became the governors of their own districts within their own provinces, which had become part of the Kongo kingdom. The governors set up their capitals in the most fertile regions of each province. This arrangement concentrated their power in the larger towns, while the rest of the populace was scattered throughout the countryside. It also allowed the king to exploit the resources of the three zones directly instead of merely taxing passing trade.

The kingdom was divided into many units called *rendas*. Each *renda* was

The *mwene Kongo* appointed the provincial governors for a period of three years. They had many fiscal, military, and administrative duties. For example, the governors had to accompany the *mwene Kongo* to war. They brought their own vassals and soldiers and enforced the same obligation on the lower chiefs. In this way the king could mobilize an army of 80,000 men. The governors had to prove their allegiance by visiting Mbanza Kongo once every three years or whenever summoned. Failure to do so was considered out-and-out rebellion.

charged a tax. The amount depended on the number of people living in the *renda*, and it could be paid in money, labor, or goods. A royal official was granted the *renda* collection for a three-year term. He kept some for himself and passed some on to the king at the capital. The taxes financed the king's household, the army, and other government expenses.

The king also collected tribute. Local people produced foodstuffs and other products from the resources available to them. Their *kanda* demanded a portion of this as tribute in return for their work. In turn, the governors of each province demanded tribute from the local *kanda*. The governors sent a portion of it to the capital, keeping some for themselves. The king sent the governors valuable gifts of products from a different zone of the kingdom. The governors maintained their regional power by distributing some of these coveted products to the local *kanda*. The king was expected to reallocate the tribute he received from the outlying provinces to the powerful *kanda* of the central province.

The governors of the coastal zone sent salt and shells as tribute to the capital. The governors in the central zone sent raffia cloth, while those of the southern, northern, and eastern areas sent copper. The system worked because people wanted the goods they could not get in their own provinces, and these goods were luxuries that most people could not afford to buy. The system also kept the entire power structure beholden to the king.

The luxury items—mainly salt and raffia cloth—were thus much in demand, and their production was encouraged. Sometimes the king even tried to control the production centers and the collection and distribution of *nzimba* shells himself.

As these items moved up the line of tribute, they became concentrated in the hands of the wealthy ruling class. Domestic animals also moved up the chain. Rural people raised chickens, goats, pigs, and sometimes cattle, but they seldom got to enjoy these foods themselves. They were given to the *kanda* and passed on through the governors to the king and other nobles, who all lived at the capital. The most valuable products of all three zones were thus to be found at the lively marketplace in Mbanza Kongo.

The ruling class benefited from this

system. They justified their gains through the economic, political, and spiritual obligations they undertook. The peasants unfortunately had no such chances. Several European visitors reported that they lived in "miserable poverty," similar to conditions in some parts of Europe at the time.

This, then, was the complex world into which the Portuguese stepped. After their arrival it was never to be the same again.

There were no donkeys, horses, or camels in the region. Merchants rode oxen along the trade routes. In this carving, the ox is mounted on the backs of two birds, and its pipe-smoking rider is protected by two magical figurines. ▶

Some historians believe that the kingdom of Kongo was not divided into regions and markets controlled by the various *kanda*. They suggest that the government was extremely centralized. Most provinces, they say, (except for Soyo and Mbata, which were formed before the kingdom was founded), were ruled by nobles appointed by the king. The *mwene Kongo* could install or remove these officials at will. They were most often members of the king's extended royal family, which ensured their loyalty. By frequently rotating the available positions, the king ensured that no one remained in power long enough to challenge the throne. When a new king came to power, he had to diplomatically replace disloyal or threatening provincial governors with his own officials. Often, rival candidates had large followings, and dispute over the valued government positions could lead to war.

The Esikongo Meet the Portuguese

In his book *Heart of Darkness*, written in 1890, Joseph Conrad described the Zaire River (or Congo, as it was then known) as follows: "Going up that river was like traveling back to the beginnings of the world, when vegetation rioted on the earth and the big trees were kings. An empty stream, a great silence, an impenetrable forest."

Four hundred years earlier, in 1483, the Portuguese sailor Diogo Cão (dee OH go kou) was the first European to see the Zaire. How must he have felt as his caravel, or small sailing ship, carefully negotiated the wide, muddy waters of the great river?

And what were the feelings of the African people who emerged from the forest to watch this strange apparition float upstream?

Diogo Cão and the Esikongo

Cão anchored his ship at Mpinda (m PIHN duh), in the Zaire estuary, in the province of Soyo. Perhaps the Esikongo believed that Cão and his crew were returning ancestors. After all, they came from the sea, which was regarded as the barrier between this life and the next. The Europeans were white, just as spirits were supposed to be. They spoke a strange language, and they brought with them marvelous gifts from "another world"—one that the Esikongo

▲ Villagers emerge from the depths of the forest along the Zaire River.

Diogo Cão

▲ Diogo Cão made these inscriptions on rocks in the Zaire estuary in 1483. They were discovered 400 years later.

had never encountered. Perhaps, however, the Esikongo simply recognized these white strangers as "foreigners," who had come for peaceful trade.

Whatever their feelings, the Esikongo came on board the caravel and traded ivory for cloth. Through sign language, the Europeans learned that the river was called Zaire and that it ran through a kingdom called Kongo. The king, the Esikongo indicated, lived several days' journey away.

Cão asked the African scouts to guide a Portuguese delegation to the king, and to bring them back at a specified time. Meanwhile, he stayed near the ship and erected a *padrao* (pah DRAH oh),

a stone pillar brought all the way from Lisbon, to commemorate his arrival.

Weeks later, after sailing another 1,100 km (700 mi) farther south, Cão returned to Mpinda, but there was still no sign of his men. Seizing four African hostages, Cão sent word to the king that these men would be returned on his next voyage if his men came back safe and sound. Cão then sailed on to Portugal.

"In the year . . .of 1482 since the birth of our Lord Jesus Christ, the most serene, most excellent, and potent prince, King D. Joao of Portugal, did order this land to be discovered and these *padraos* to be set up by D. Cão, an esquire of his household."

— *Inscription on the padrao erected by Cão at the mouth of the Zaire River.*

In Lisbon the hostages were treated kindly. They met the king of Portugal, were entertained by the nobility, and eventually converted to Christianity. These men now wore rich European clothing and spoke some Portuguese. After two years in Portugal, they had changed a great deal from when they first traded on board Cão's caravel.

In 1485, Diogo Cão returned to the Zaire, found his men, and released his hostages. The former hostages were now personal witnesses to the wonders of the "other world" and functioned as able interpreters. They impressed the king with their reports. In keeping with tradition, the *mwene kongo* sent gifts of ivory and raffia cloth to Diogo Cão. He hoped to include the newcomers in the ancient system of tribute.

Cão died on the return journey to Portugal, but the *mwene Kongo*'s diplomacy was not ignored. The Portuguese king, seeing a great opportunity for trade, ordered a mass assault on Kongo. It was not to be achieved with weapons, but with trade goods, technology, and, above all, the Catholic faith.

Christianity for the Esikongo

In March 1491, a fleet of Portuguese ships arrived at the mouth of the Zaire. This time, it brought priests, missionaries, carpenters, masons, tools, instruments, horses, clothes, ornaments, and religious items—everything the Portuguese needed to infiltrate the Kongo culture with their own. They even brought women, who were directed to teach the Esikongo the arts of Portuguese housekeeping!

The ships anchored again at Mpinda, and the captain presented the district governor, or *mwene Soyo*, with gifts. The *mwene Soyo* greeted the Europeans by touching both hands to the ground and putting them to his head—a sacred gesture of the *mbumba* cult. Then he organized a great festival of singing, drumming, and dancing. The Portuguese fired their muskets in a show of power. Finally the *mwene Soyo* and his son were baptized.

The scene was repeated at Mbanza Kongo, the capital, a week's march from Mpinda. The Portuguese were

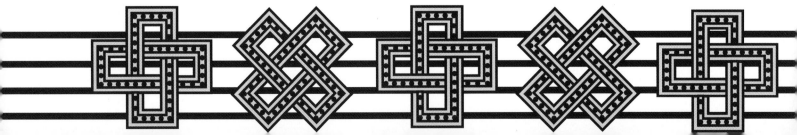

41

accompanied by a singing, dancing throng of hundreds of people. They were led to the *mwene Kongo*

himself, Nzinga a Nkuwu (n ZIHN guh ah n KOO woo). He sat on a throne inlaid with ivory and raised on a great platform. He wore a loincloth, a royal cap, and copper bracelets. A zebra tail— the badge of kingship—hung from his left shoulder.

The Portuguese presented the king with brocades, velvet and silk fabrics, horsetails mounted in silver, gold and silver trinkets, magnificent

garments, and a cage of red pigeons. The king greeted the Portuguese with ritual *mbumba* cult gestures. Then he asked to be baptized.

The Portuguese priests—who, after all, had come thousands of miles for just this purpose—could not believe their luck. In West Africa, their missions had met with little success. But here was an African culture that seemed to welcome Christianity with open arms!

On May 3, 1491, the *mwene Kongo*, most of his court, and hundreds of commoners were baptized. The nobles took Portuguese names and titles. Nzinga a

◀ Once Christianity took hold in Kongo, many crucifixes like this one were made, in which Christ was depicted as an African, and often as a woman.

◀ The *nwene Kongo* is baptized.

Nkuwu became King Joao (jou) [John] I, after the Portuguese king. His son, the governor of the province of Nsundi, was now called Afonso—a name that, as one chronicler noted, "he was to make glorious." Immediately after the ceremony, building began on a stone church.

The Portuguese believed they had accomplished their mission, but the Esikongo actually had their own reasons for accepting Christianity. Some historians believe that they saw baptism into Christianity as an initiation into another cult headed by the Portuguese king. In this light, baptism would not have seemed strange to the Esikongo at all.

In addition, the *mwene Kongo* was very interested in trade. Indeed, he controlled all trade in the kingdom and was eager to impress the Portuguese with Kongo's suitability as a trading partner. What better way to achieve this than by "taking on" the strangers' religion?

The Esikongo believed in a supreme god, the creator, called *Nzambi a Mpugu*. But since he was invisible and inaccessible, he could not be worshipped or even represented in any form. Christianity strengthened this belief in a divine being. A host of lesser gods and spirits of deceased ancestors governed the individual's life. People wore many idols and fetishes. Some also worshipped the sun, moon, or stars. Most people consulted an oracle before making decisions or embarking on a journey.

The *mwene Kongo* was also about to help his son Afonso put down a rebellion in the Nsundi province. He wanted to enlist Portuguese aid in this matter and knew that once he was baptized, it would be hard for the Portuguese to refuse him.

Aid From the Portuguese

King Joao was right. The Portuguese felt obliged to help a brother in Christ. Thus a black army, aided by a few white soldiers, marched to battle under the Christian banner. The Portuguese soldiers wore armor, used crossbows, and were immensely skillful at sword fighting. The Esikongo warriors, also skilled swordsmen, carried buffalo-hide shields. They opened the battle with volleys of arrows, followed by a charge into hand-to-hand combat. The Portuguese also helped by drawing their ship up river, near to the island where the battle was raging. From there, they launched their ship's artillery at the enemy.

Not surprisingly, the *mwene Kongo* returned to the capital in triumph. In gratitude, he settled the Portuguese in their own section of town, near his palace. For a time, peace and friendship ruled. Doors were left open, it was said, with no need for guards. The 500-year association between the Esikongo and the Portuguese had begun.

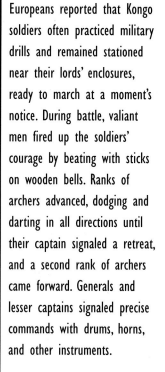

Europeans reported that Kongo soldiers often practiced military drills and remained stationed near their lords' enclosures, ready to march at a moment's notice. During battle, valiant men fired up the soldiers' courage by beating with sticks on wooden bells. Ranks of archers advanced, dodging and darting in all directions until their captain signaled a retreat, and a second rank of archers came forward. Generals and lesser captains signaled precise commands with drums, horns, and other instruments.

In the late fifteenth century, the gun was still a very primitive weapon. A few Portuguese soldiers in Kongo might have had matchlock muskets. These were deadly but took a long time to reload and had a short range. They were probably not of much use in African warfare. European soldiers relied on arrows and pikes until the 1680s, when the flintlock musket was developed. Only then did the gun became the main weapon in Africa.

Tribute and Trade—
A Delicate Balance

Afonso: The True Believer

When King Joao I died, his wife, baptized Eleanor, kept his death secret, for she was a good Christian, and she wished her Christian son, Afonso, to become king. In truth, his brother Mpanzu claimed the throne, and Mpanzu despised the Christian faith.

Thus, for three days following Joao's death, Eleanor allowed no one near the king's chambers. In great haste, she sent runners to the province of Nsundi, where Afonso was governor. And each ran his distance, passing on his message to the next, until word of his father's death reached Afonso. And in one day and two nights, he accomplished with marvelous speed, being carried by porters, the great distance and suddenly appeared in the city.

Now, together with the death of King Joao, was announced the succession to the throne of Dom Afonso. But his rival Mpanzu had many followers. They hated the Christians and believed that they had brought ill upon the land. How could their *kanda* compete with the wondrous gifts brought by the white strangers, which only the king could buy? Not only this, but these Christians ruled that a man might have only one wife! For this reason, the

◀ In Kongo, the king or wealthy nobles often traveled in a litter, carried by four slaves. For long distances, a relay system was organized. One team would cover a certain distance, and then another team would take over. In this way, King Afonso was able to cover the great distance from Mbanza Nsundi to Mbanza Kongo in only one day and two nights to claim the throne.

Christians supported Afonso, who was baptized and who was the son of Eleanor, the king's principal wife.

Mpanzu and his followers were outraged. How could a man build his family and become prosperous with only one wife? Indeed, with their new ideas these

In this sixteenth century drawing a Portuguese captain kneels before King Afonso, whose African subjects prostrate themselves on the ground. Afonso is shown wearing European clothing, which he often did, especially on ceremonial occasions. The crown may be the artist's addition. ▶

strangers from foreign shores were undermining the very foundations of the ancient Kongo cults and traditions. Mpanzu vowed to seize the throne and rid the land of these troublesome people.

He then collected a great force, to the number of nearly 200,000 men, and came armed against Afonso. Dom Afonso awaited him in the royal city with those few friends—some 10,000—who had agreed to defend the place. But

they proved doubtful and timid on account of the great army Mpanzu had brought with him.

Afonso was resolute. Those who wished to surrender should do so, he cried. He would fight in the name of God, who would protect him and his followers! And they received further encouragement from the aged lord of Soyo. "Behold, my age is now 100 years," he said, "and yet I take arms, being zealous for the religion that I have adopted. And do you, who are in the flower of your age, show timidity, and so little loyalty to your lawful sovereign?"

At this moment came a heavenly vision in the form of a bright and beautiful light. At the sight of this, Afonso fell on his knees in tears, lifting his eyes and hands to heaven, in a state of rapture from what he saw. All present did the same and were blinded for a time by the brightness of the light. Then, by degrees, lifting their eyes to heaven, they saw five flaming swords that remained transfixed in a circle for the space of an hour.

This vision greatly strengthened the minds of the citizens, even while it struck terror into the hearts of the opposing army. Notwithstanding, Mpanzu ordered his army to block the only passage from the royal city. On this path there was a shallow marsh, and here Mpanzu's soldiers drove sharp stakes, covering them with water, so that the enemy might suddenly be ensnared by them and perish.

In the early morning, Mpanzu led the assault with furious energy on the north side of the city, where the great plain forms an open battleground. Here, Dom Afonso and his handful of men were ranged against the pagans. But before they could fight, Mpanzu's men launched their arrows and fled!

The next day, Mpanzu returned to the assault in the same place and again—at the moment of attack—seemed to flee in fear!

Afonso was amazed. What cowards were these? Why had he been so easily granted this victory? Afonso's men had captured some enemy soldiers. From them, they learned that Afonso's victory was the result of a miracle. At first, the enemy had been confused and blinded by the dazzling vision of a lady in white. Then they had been put to flight by a knight riding a great white steed and bearing a red cross on his breast.

On hearing this, Dom Afonso sent word to Mpanzu that these visions were the Virgin Mary, the Mother of God, and Saint James, who were sent from God to his aid. If Mpanzu would become a Christian, said Afonso's message, he too could receive similar favors.

Mpanzu would not in any way consent to this. He spent the night arranging for the conquest of the city from two positions. Part of his army he sent to the narrow pass where he had placed stakes in the marshes. With the other, led by himself, he attempted to reach the city by way of the river, where there were no guards. He made his first onslaught but was easily routed. Hoping to push on to the other side of the city, while his enemies were defending the pass, Mpanzu fell into a trap, for those who were in the city, hearing from their scouts that Mpanzu was coming their way, hastened there to repulse him. They fought with such fury against him that, being overcome by fright, he rushed headlong into the marshy ambush covered with stakes that he himself had prepared. And there, almost maddened with pain, the points of the stakes being poisoned and penetrating his flesh, Mpanzu's life ended.

With this victory and the death of his rival, King Afonso was freed from further opposition. At once, he set about building the Church of the Holy Cross, so called after the flaming swords seen in the sky. To set an example for his people, he was the first to carry stones on his shoulders for the foundation. The building was quickly raised, and a great number of nobles asked for baptism.

Besides this, King Afonso assembled the governors from the different provinces. He told them publicly that whoever possessed idols contrary to the Christian religion must give them up or be burned and receive no pardon. Thus in less than a month were brought to the court all the sorcery books, magic writings, and idols that had been worshipped as gods. Truly, great numbers of these things were collected—winged dragons, serpents of horrible shape, large goats, tigers, and various monstrous animals. The more they were ugly and deformed, the more they had been held in honor.

Now the king commanded that to the same place where he had conquered Mpanzu every person should bring a piece of wood. A great pile was raised, and there the idols were cast in and burned. Then Afonso assembled all the people and gave them crosses and images of the saints, which he had received from the Portuguese. He commanded each of his lords to build a church and to erect crosses in the cities of the provinces that they ruled.

In this manner, in process of time, the Catholic faith took root in those regions. And when King Afonso was near death, he spoke of the Christian religion with great love and trust. He left no doubt that the cross and the true faith were forever imprinted on his heart.

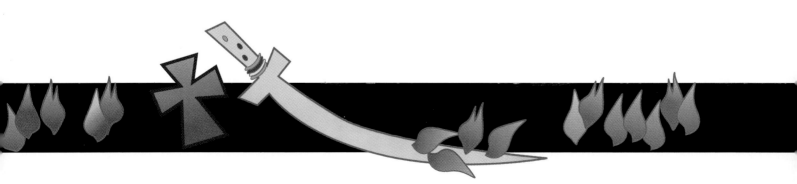

The Historical Record

This account of Afonso's rise to power in 1506 is adapted from a book written by Filippo Pigafetta in 1591 and translated into English in 1597. Pigafetta's work was, in turn, drawn from the accounts of Duarte (dwart) Lopes, (loh-PEZ) a sailor who voyaged to Luanda in 1578. Lopes spent 12 years in the kingdom of Kongo. He was knighted there and served as Kongo's ambassador to Rome. His account gave historians one of the fullest and most accurate records of the region at that time.

King Afonso I remains one of the most fascinating figures of the kingdom's turbulent history. In fact, a missionary, writing in 1889, claimed that "a Negro from the Kongo knows the names of only three kings—that of the reigning monarch, that of his predecessor, and that of Dom Afonso I."

What kind of a man was Afonso? Why did he so eagerly accept the Christian faith, and what kind of kingdom did he envision? Rui d'Aguiar (rwee dah-GWAHR), a Catholic priest in the Kongo, provides some insight into these questions in a letter he wrote to the king of Portugal in 1516.

May your Highness be informed that Afonso's Christian life is such that he appears to me not as a man but as an angel. . . . For I assure your Highness that it is he who instructs us; better than we, he knows the Prophets and the Gospel of Our Lord Jesus Christ and all the lives of the saints. . . . I must say, Lord, that he does nothing but study and that many times he falls asleep over his books. . . . When he gives audience or when he dispenses justice, his words are inspired by God . . .

▲ Afonso dictated many letters to the king of Portugal. Shown here are the last lines of a letter with his official signature.

In 1791, Daniel Defoe (author of *Robinson Crusoe*) wrote a popular book called *Travels of Captain Singleton*. His book astonished nineteenth-century readers because it seemed to have foreseen the discoveries made then in the Congo by the explorer Henry Morton Stanley. In fact, Defoe carries his hero, Captain Singleton, through exactly the same scenes and events that Duarte Lopes experienced when he visited Kongo in 1578, and which were translated by Filippo Pigafetta in 1591. Clearly, Defoe had read this important historical work.

As Pigafetta relates, Afonso began his reign by destroying the traditional idols and replacing them with sacred objects of the Catholic faith. He also built several churches in Mbanza Kongo.

Afonso was a progressive man for his time. He developed an education policy for the children of nobles. By 1516, more than a thousand boys attended school in Mbanza Kongo, where they learned reading, writing, and the articles of the Catholic faith. One of the king's sisters also directed schools for girls—a truly innovative program.

Afonso learned to speak and write Portuguese. He wore Portuguese clothing and modeled his court on the court in Lisbon. (By the sixteenth century, Kongo nobles had adopted Portuguese titles, such as "principes, duques, marquezes" [princes, dukes, marquises].) Afonso kept up an endless stream of letters to "his brother" the king, demanding more priests and, especially, more teachers for his schools.

Afonso sent many young men to Portugal to be educated. One of them became the principal of a college in Lisbon. Another—Afonso's own son Henrique—became a bishop and returned to the kingdom to perform his religious duties there.

A Balancing Act

Afonso inherited a situation that had begun with his father, King Joao I. Joao had defined the Christian religion as a new cult—one that fit in very well with the existing Kongo traditions. But most of the nobles were also baptized and therefore belonged to the same cult. King Joao failed to make the new cult his exclusive realm, and so had to share his status and power with his titleholders.

In addition, King Joao had very little to offer the Portuguese. They came looking for gold, and the best he could offer was ivory and palm cloth. So the Portuguese reduced the value of their own gifts, which in turn reduced the king's status at the peak of the tribute system.

Many of King Joao's chief titleholders—those important men and

Afonso's educational policy paid off. Members of the Esikongo ruling class were able to write letters in Portuguese, using either paper (which was very expensive) or banana leaves. Court testimonies, records of inquests, certificates of office, and church proceedings were recorded. Literacy made better and faster communications possible to the interior of the kingdom and also directly to Europe. Kongo schools were so good that Miguel de Castro, a seventeenth-century nobleman educated there, could hold his own in Europe as a recognized author of Latin poetry.

In 1495, King Joao I of Kongo threw the Christians—led by his own son, Afonso—out of Mbanza Kongo. Afonso became governor of Nsundi. Many Portuguese followed this Christian prince and became his supporters when he was king and moved to the capital, where he revived the Christian faith. Most Esikongo were baptized and actively sought the sacrament. They took saints' names, learned Christian songs and prayers, and celebrated Christian holidays. At the same time, they continued to believe that their ancestors could affect their lives. To them, the Christian saints they worshipped were much like the "spirits" they had worshipped before the arrival of Christianity.

women of the *kanda* and *kitome* groups and the lords of the various provinces—were completely opposed to the Christians. After all, the Catholic priests threatened the status of the *kitome*, who were spiritual leaders or "priests" in their own right. And when the Catholic priests demanded that the king keep only his principal wife, the Kongo officials saw their own security crumbling, for the king's lesser wives were almost always related to the titleholders and created their bond to the royal house.

It was thus easy for Afonso's brother Mpanzu to gain followers and build his huge army. Even though Mpanzu was defeated by Afonso, his followers formed a discontented, bristling group that continually threatened the king's power.

Afonso, however, was in a stronger position than his father had been. For several years, he had been governor of the province of Nsundi, northeast of the capital. From there, he controlled the trade route to the mining region north of the Zaire River, where copper was collected. When he became

Copper was sold in the form of arm rings. Between 1506 and 1511, Afonso exported 5,200 such arm rings.

king, Afonso was able to offer the Portuguese this copper, which was highly valued in Europe. In return, their gifts to him increased in value. Afonso distributed these gifts among the governors of the provinces, thus gradually winning their support.

Afonso personally manipulated the trade of the kingdom. He not only controlled the copper route but also held the monopoly on the valuable *nzimbu* shells collected at Luanda. With the copper, the shells, and ivory, palm cloth, skins, and honey collected through the tribute system, he could purchase more goods from the Portuguese traders than anyone else.

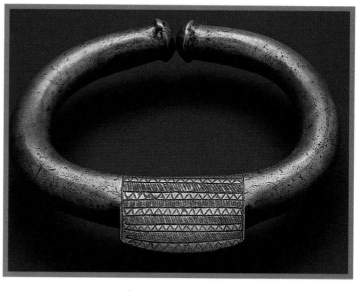

▲ Copper arm rings similar to this one were a valuable form of currency in Kongo.

Afonso's power thus hung delicately in the balance. As long as he could supply the Portuguese with valuable trade goods, he could maintain his authority as king. As soon as that position was threatened, he would tumble.

Black Gold

As in many other parts of Africa, slavery was common in the kingdom of Kongo. Slaves were usually war captives, criminals, or other undesirables. Sometimes, people would pawn themselves or a relative into slavery to pay off a debt. Slaves usually worked as soldiers, laborers, or domestic servants. In many cases, because they were politically neutral and had lost their tribal ties, slaves were useful in government and could attain highly responsible positions. In Kongo, they might be messengers, nobles, and trusted merchants, trading for their masters.

Slaves in Africa were usually not far removed from their homelands. They were largely familiar with the culture that had enslaved them. Their labor benefited the local African economy, and they could marry, own property, and often buy or otherwise earn their freedom. This was a very different system from the type of slavery established by the Portuguese soon after their explorations of the west African coast had begun.

The Beginnings

In 1415, Prince Henry of Portugal, known as Henry the Navigator, had been a Crusader in the North African Muslim port city of Ceuta (say-OO-tah). There he saw camel caravans arrive, heavily laden with gold. Where did the gold come from? the prince inquired. From the fabulously wealthy kingdom of Mali, south of the Sahara, he was told. Prince Henry determined to find the source of this African gold by sailing down the west coast of the continent.

At this time, the Europeans had also developed a taste for sugar, which had fetched top prices ever since Crusaders in the Middle East tasted it for the first time. So the Portuguese were also searching for tropical islands like Madeira (mah DEE ruh), far off the western coast of present-day Morocco, where sugar cane could be grown.

In the Middle Ages, the European economy had been mostly based on spices and other rare goods obtained from the Far East. The trade routes passed over land and by sea from China and Malaysia via India, converging on the city of Constantinople (Istanbul). In 1453, the city—the vital link between Europe and the east—fell to the Turks. The trade routes were closed to European merchants and the prices of goods skyrocketed. Now, Europeans searched not only for gold and new lands suitable for planting sugar cane, but also for new routes to the East. These factors were the cata-

In this eighteenth-century drawing of Kongo life, an African slave carries a parasol of woven grass for his African master. ▶

> "The noble spirit of this Prince was ever urging him . . . to carry out very great deeds. . . . He had also a wish to know the land that lay beyond the isles of Canary and that cape called Bojador, for up to his time, neither by writings, nor by the memory of man, was known with certainty the nature of the land beyond that Cape."
> —*Gomes Eannes de Anzurara,* Discovery and Conquest of Guinea, *1453*

lysts that triggered the explosive age of exploration.

The Italian explorer Christopher Columbus thought he could reach the East by sailing west. But the Portuguese believed that they might reach the East by sailing around Africa to India. The journey around Africa had never before been attempted. How big was Africa? How long would the voyage take? No one knew. But the lure of gold, new sugar plantations, and great profits to be made from trade with India and China was irresistible.

Starting around 1419, Prince Henry financed one voyage after another. By 1433, he had sent 15 expeditions down Africa's northwestern coast, but each turned back at the infamous Cape Bojador (boh hah DOR). They were afraid to continue, for, it was said, ". . . beyond this cape there is no race of men nor place of inhabitants . . . while the currents

▲ In this fifteenth-century painting, Prince Henry of Portugal leads troops against the Muslim city of Ceuta, on Africa's northern shore. As a Crusader, Henry received much geographical and historical information about Africa from the Moors. When his campaigns were over, he set up a map-making institute and a center of worldwide exploration. Prince Henry financed several voyages of exploration down the west coast of Africa.

The Portuguese made their way down the west coast of Africa in ships like this sixteenth-century caravel. ▶

are so terrible that no ship having once passed . . . will ever
be able to return."

At last, in 1434, a captain named Gil Eannes (zheel ahnsh)
rounded the cape and landed on the African coast. The spell
was broken, and now each new voyage ventured farther south.

In 1442, a few West Africans were captured as "souvenirs" and
taken to Lisbon. It soon became fashionable for middle- and
upper-class Europeans to own black servants, and over the next
60 years, the slow trickle of slaves from West Africa to Europe
became a flood. By 1550,
African slaves made up at
least 10 percent of the population of Lisbon.

By 1731, when this French map was
drawn, Europeans had gained greater
knowledge of the kingdom of Kongo or
"Royaume de Congo" in French. ▼

While the Portuguese had
not come to Africa in
search of slaves, they were
familiar with the practice
of slavery. In fact,
European merchants used
slaves from North Africa
and Russia to work sugar
plantations on various
Mediterranean islands. The
uninhabited islands of
Principe (PREEN see pay)
and São Tomé (sou toh-
MAY), off the central west

◄ This Portuguese map, drawn in
1502, shows extensive knowledge of
West Africa. The kingdom of Kongo is
marked south of the Zaire River.

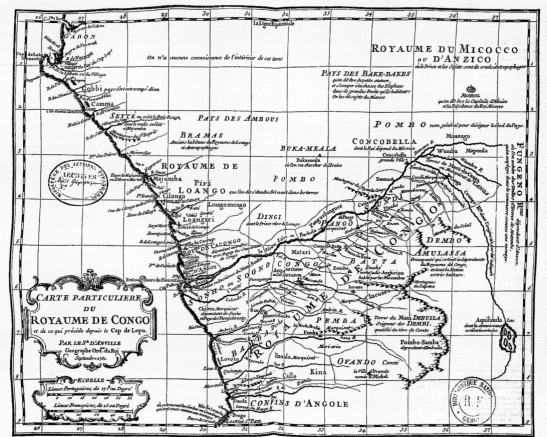

African coast, turned out to be perfect for growing sugar cane. To the Portuguese, it was logical to use slaves captured from the mainland to work these new plantations. And once Columbus had reached the Americas in 1492, it was a further logical step to establish the Portuguese plantation system in the "New World."

By 1482, gold and slaves were being exported from the Portuguese trading fort of El Mina on the Gold Coast (Ghana). By 1483, Diogo Cão had reached the mouth of the Zaire River. Only five years later, Bartholomeu Dias reached the Cape of Good Hope. And in 1498, Vasco da Gama rounded the Cape and sailed for Calicutt in India. The Portuguese had found their African gold. They had found islands for their sugar plantations, and they had found their trade route to the East. On the way, they had discovered a trade that was to prove more lucrative than gold, sugar, or spices—the slave trade, so profitable that its human cargo came to be called "black gold."

Afonso's Monopoly Threatened

The economy of the kingdom of Kongo was based mainly on the tribute system, in which war captives and goods such as cloth, ivory, skins, domestic animals, and foodstuffs were exchanged. The king received enough revenue from these

MONEY, MONEY, MONEY

Standard-size vessels contained specific numbers of *nzimbu* shells, ranging from 40 to 20,000. Large shells were ten times more valuable than small shells.

Values in the mid-seventeenth century were the following (dollar amounts are based on silver values in January 1995).

1 *funda* = 1,000 big shells = 100 *reis* = 58 grams of silver = $113
1 *lukufu* = 10,000 big shells = 1,000 *reis* = 580 grams of silver = $226
1 *kofo* = 20,000 big shells = 2,000 *reis* = 1160 grams of silver = $452

Afonso I paid a stonemason as much as one *kofo* per day! A *reis* (rays) was a silver coin used not for purchasing goods but as a way of keeping accounts. The value of goods was convverted to *reis* so that a trader knew the exact value of his holdings in stock without actually having the goods.

goods and from trade tolls and taxes to maintain his authority. He also monopolized the *nzimbu* shell money collected at Luanga.

The Portuguese brought goods with them that upset the carefully balanced give-and-take of the tribute system. Red parasols, gilt mirrors, brass hairpins, and other trinkets soon became hot items among the Esikongo. In exchange, the Portuguese accepted ivory, copper, cloth, skins, and slaves. From the start of the Kongo-Portuguese relationship, Kongo had exported slaves to the sugar plantations on the island of São Tomé, which had become one of the leading sugar producers in the world. As the demand for sugar in Europe escalated, the plantations on the island and in the Portuguese colony of Brazil grew in size and number. Managers could not get enough slaves to do the work, and those they bought usually died after three to five years. Thus there was a constant need to replace them. By 1516, Kongo was already exporting 4,000 slaves a year, and that number was to rise continuously.

Touch and Go

Afonso must have been very disappointed in the Portuguese. He cer-

São Tomé—Capital of Portuguese West Africa

Portuguese sailors reached the uninhabited island of São Tomé in 1472, and official settlement began in 1473. The climate there was deadly to Europeans. The earliest settlement consisted of 600 exiled Jewish children, sent to settle or die. Those who did survive intermarried with Africans and Portuguese. Soon a mixed plantation colony developed that became the seat of Portuguese government in the Gulf of Guinea. Its authority stretched from the fort of El Mina (in Ghana) to the colony of Angola, south of Kongo, which included the kingdom of Ndongo and which the Portuguese founded in 1571. The Tomistas, as the inhabitants of São Tomé were called, were extremely active in all the Portuguese ventures in Africa. On São Tomé, a common creole language was spoken. This mixture of Portuguese and African languages was spoken in trading communities throughout the Gulf region. In the nineteenth century, it was gradually replaced by Pidgin English, still spoken today. Pidgin English contains many Portuguese words, reflecting its origins on São Tomé.

tainly desired trade contacts with them. He was also a truly devout Christian and sincerely believed that the Portuguese and Esikongo cultures could flourish side by side, each bene-fiting from the other. Yet he com-plained in his letters to the Portuguese king that the Portuguese soldiers did not fight well, or carry out their assignments. In other words, they were of little use to him in his various wars. In a letter written in 1526, Afonso also complained bitterly that the provincial governors and chiefs were becoming richer in European goods than he. Now, having no need of the king, they refused tribute and rebelled.

Afonso could only maintain his posi-tion as *mwene Kongo* through the trib-ute system. He had to contend with the mounting Portuguese pressure for more and more slaves in exchange for the goods he needed to keep his title-holders in allegiance and for the priests, artisans, and teachers he badly needed and so often requested.

By Kongo law, only war captives could be sold into slavery, and there were very few available. Afonso raided a nearby region for slaves, but he had no guns and no standing

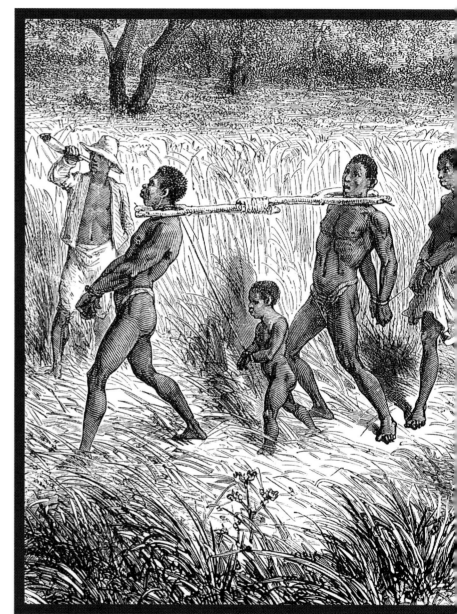

army. Certain Kongo individuals were kidnapping Kongo's own people for sale and dealing directly with the Portuguese. Meanwhile the Portuguese themselves were raiding the interior. Even the Portuguese priests, whom Afonso had so admired, were heavily involved in the slave trade.

Afonso now turned to his old contacts in the Nsundi region, where he had been governor. They had kept the copper route from the Tio (TEE oh) region north of Nsundi to the coast open for years. Now they were able to supply slaves along this route, which passed through Afonso's capital at Mbanza Kongo. By supplying the Portuguese with slaves, Afonso was able to maintain his power at the top of the tribute system. In addition, the Tio people demanded *nzimbu* shell money for their slaves. Afonso held the monopoly on the shells, which prevented the Portuguese from direct purchase with the Tio.

◀ Traders known as *pombeiros*, who were usually Afro-Portuguese of mixed blood, traveled far into the interior to buy slaves from African traders. Such journeys could last two years or more. The captives—men, women, and children—wore heavy yokes to prevent escape. Many Africans died before they ever reached the Portuguese ships at the coast.

In 1526, Afonso wrote to the king of Portugal about the slave trade: "We cannot estimate how great the damage is, because the merchants capture daily our own subjects, sons of our noblemen, vassals, and relatives . . . and cause them to be sold. . . . It is our will that in these kingdoms there should not be any trade in slaves or market for slaves." Some historians believe Afonso was writing about Kongo. Others suggest that he was referring to Ndongo, Kongo's rival in trade. He would have wanted the slave trade in Ndongo to cease in order to benefit his own kingdom.

There are no definite statistics on the number of slaves exported from Kongo, but rough estimates suggest that about 350,000 people were taken between 1500 and 1600. In all, 2 million or more Angolans were bought or captured by Portuguese, French, British, Brazilian, and Dutch merchants.

Afonso was at times threatened by attempts to seize the throne. He even narrowly escaped assassination in 1540. His position in Kongo had been threatened by the Portuguese and the slave trade. Yet he strengthened his power and used it effectively, ensuring the loyalty of his title-holders. He ignored the Christian rule on monogamy and placed his sons in important government positions. Through tribute, he drew in many new regions, expanding the kingdom to almost double its size.

He established Christianity throughout the region, and developed a highly literate upper class through his education system.

When Afonso died in 1543, he is said to have been forgotten by the king in Portugal. It is ironic that Afonso has gone down in history as Kongo's greatest king—the one who is remembered to this day above all others. In fact, some historians call the reign of Dom Afonso I the "Golden Age" of Kongo.

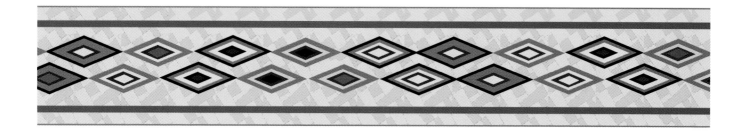

Prayers for Peace

Beatriz Kimpa Vita: The Black Joan of Arc

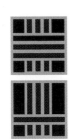

The slender young girl lay in the throes of death. Even her parents had given up hope that she might live, for she had been ill for many days. But just when it seemed she might breathe no more, Dona Beatriz had a vision. A Catholic priest appeared to her, saying he was Saint Anthony, sent by God through her to restore the kingdom of Kongo. He threatened those who would try to oppose him with severe punishment, but he promised peace, power, and glory to those who followed him.

Dona Beatriz believed that she had died, and that her own soul had been replaced by Saint Anthony. Without knowing how, she felt herself revive. She arose from her sickbed and revealed her vision to her parents. She must go to São Salvador and preach, she said. She must teach the people, pray for peace, and thus hasten the recovery of the kingdom.

Just as Saint Anthony had commanded, Dona Beatriz gave away all her few possessions. From then on, she led the life of a holy woman, and soon she had gathered many followers.

White people, Dona Beatriz preached, were made from a soft, claylike rock. But Africans came from a great fig tree. The leaders of her group of followers proudly wore crowns of the braided fibers of this tree, which they saw as the emblem of their faith. The Kongo, Dona Beatriz taught, was the true Holy Land, and the founders of Christianity were Negroes. Christ had been born in São Salvador and baptized in Nsundi. The Virgin Mary had been born of an African slave woman.

Dona Beatriz predicted a golden age. She would reoccupy Mbanza Kongo—now called São Salvador—which had been destroyed by enemy invasions. The roots of fallen trees would transform themselves into gold and silver. The ruins of the city would reveal treasure troves of precious stones and metals. And all the rich products of the whites would come to those who followed this new faith and worked to rebuild the kingdom. Kongo would revive in all its former glory!

Wherever Dona Beatriz went, her women disciples cleared her path. And when she walked these paths, it was said that twisted trees suddenly grew straight. People wished to touch her and to receive her blessed touch in return. They gave her their cloaks to cover her head and fought over food and drink that she had touched.

Every Friday, Dona Beatriz imitated the death of Christ. She claimed that she "died and went to heaven," where she dined with God and pleaded the cause of the Negroes, especially the restoration of the

◀ Father Barnardo da Gallo painted this portrait of Beatriz Kimpa Vita. "This young woman was about twenty-two years old. She was rather slender and fine-featured. Externally she appeared very devout. She spoke with gravity, and seemed to weigh each word. She foretold the future and predicted, among other things, that the day of Judgement was near."
—Father Lorenzo da Lucca, 1706

kingdom. On Saturdays, she was "born again," returning to earth to bring God's messages to her people. Dona Beatriz also wished to imitate the Virgin Mary and to have a son who would become a savior. A son was indeed born to her, a son whom she claimed came from heaven.

The Esikongo believed that their prayers had been answered. After years of pain and suffering, God had at last cast his benevolent eye upon them. Dona Beatriz was His messenger, and the kingdom would find salvation through her.

Dona Beatriz prepared to reoccupy the abandoned city of São Salvador. She commanded the nobles to follow her there and to recognize her as their spiritual leader. From their numbers, she said, she would choose one to be the *mwene Kongo*.

And thus it happened that São Salvador was soon repopulated. Some went there to worship Dona Beatriz, the saint; others to see the rebuilt capital. Some merely went to

◀ This nineteenth-century wooden image from Kongo idealizes feminine beauty as a mother tenderly cradles her infant's head in her hands. The figure was believed to have healing powers for gynecological illnesses.

watch, while others believed they could miraculously recover their health. Some came with political ambitions, and some were returning home.

In São Salvador, Dona Beatriz Kimpa Vita pronounced herself the spiritual leader of the kingdom. Already present in the capital city was a man named Pedro Constantinho da Silva. He was a noble of high position who was making preparations for King Pedro IV to leave his island of refuge and reenter the city. Seeing here a chance for his own advancement, da Silva too joined Dona Beatriz's movement and converted to her beliefs. In return, she crowned him the "true" king of Kongo.

While many Esikongo were thus enthralled with their Saint Anthony, there were those who opposed Beatriz. The ruler of the southern province of Mbamba wished to rid his domain of her doctrine. With holy zeal, he took up a great cross and traveled with it throughout the huge region, rounding up the devils incarnate and purging the people of their unholy beliefs.

The Catholic priests in the kingdom also became increasingly outraged. Fathers Bernardo da Gallo and Lorenzo da Lucca, both missionaries of the Italian Capuchin order, charged that this "Saint Anthony" was undermining their teachings. Dona Beatriz is a fraud! they claimed. She had changed the words of sacred Catholic hymns to suit her own purposes. And what kind of a heretic was she, who claimed to be Saint Anthony—a man—yet also claimed the virgin birth of her own son?

The missionaries demanded that King Pedro take action against Dona Beatriz. At first, Pedro held back, for he did not wish to alienate the people who believed in her. But in the end, the Capuchin friars prevailed. On July 2, 1706, Bernardo da Gallo and Lorenzo da Lucca were witnesses as Dona Beatriz, her "Angel Guardian" (a disciple named Barros), and her newborn son were brought to trial.

The royal messengers stood in the center of the great multitude of people and gave a signal with bells that they carried in each hand. At once, the people fell back, and in the space appeared the judge. He was clad from head to foot in a black mantle and wore a black hat. The culprits were led before him. The young woman, who carried her child in her arms, was filled with fear and dread. She sat on the bare ground before the crowd, her head lowered.

In solemn tones, as befitted the occasion, the judge began to speak. First he eulogized the king. Then he spoke at length, giving proof of his own worthiness as a judge.

The crowd remained deadly silent. The judge paused. Now, at last, the sentence would be pronounced upon the culprits.

Under the false name of Saint Anthony, the judge proclaimed, this woman—Dona Beatriz Kimpa Vita—had deceived the people with her heresies and falsehoods. Consequently the king, her lord, and the royal councils condemned her to be burned at the stake, together with her child and her disciple, Barros, known as Saint John. Father da Lucca found this too great a cruelty and persuaded the king to let the baby live.

Amid the great tumult of the crowd, Dona Beatriz and Barros were led to the stake. She cried out her willingness to recant, to take back the words that had led her thus far, but it was too late. With the name of Jesus upon her lips, she was thrown upon a great pile of wood. Torches set the pyre alight, and soon there was nothing left of Dona Beatriz but bones and embers. The next day, men came and burned even those poor bones yet again, reducing them to fine ashes. No trace whatsoever of Dona Beatriz should remain.

Poor Saint Anthony, who was in the habit of dying and rising again, this time died but did not rise again. Thus did Father Bernardo da Gallo comment upon the tragic death of Beatriz Kimpa Vita, which he had helped to bring about.

◀ This mask was worn by the ritual priest, or *nganga*, during official ceremonies or when searching for the soul of an ill person. Perhaps Beatriz wore such a mask in her role as an *nganga*. The white color is associated with death.

Gourds of many shapes and sizes were used in Kongo. This one has a pouring spout and is decorated with nails. ▶

Catholicism and Kongo Cults

Why did the Esikongo peasants so fully believe in Beatriz Kimpa Vita's religious movement, which historians call Antonianism, after Saint Anthony? Did they not have strong enough beliefs of their own to carry them through the dark ages of Kongo?

The answers to these questions are not hard to find. After all, Beatriz accepted and preached many Christian ideas, and by the early eighteenth century, the Esikongo had been exposed to Christianity for over 200 years. Beatriz was against vice and superstition. She generally abhorred the same sins as did the Catholic fathers. And just like the Catholics, she established her own church and sent out missionaries to preach her message.

There were, however, major differences between Beatriz and the European Catholics. She told her people not to worship the cross, because it was responsible for Christ's death. She rejected Catholic baptism, confession, and prayer, and she made polygamy (several wives to one man) legal. She opposed the white missionaries in Kongo and accused them of preventing the work of her "black saints."

Scholars of Kongo culture have placed Beatriz firmly within the framework of the *kimpasi* cult. Before being possessed by Saint Anthony, she had been an *nganga marinda*—a spiritual *kimpasi* leader who had the power to communicate directly with ancestors and other spirits. In this cult, it was normal for members to symbolically "die" and be possessed by spirits who then inhabited their bodies. It was perfectly acceptable, then, for her to be possessed by Saint Anthony in the same way.

In Esikongo ideals of justice, people's intentions were as a important as their actions. A man who killed another might be pardoned if it was felt that his intentions were for the good of the community and not for himself. Dona Beatriz argued that the Catholic sacraments of marriage, baptism, and confession served no purpose. God would know the believer's intentions without needing to hear formal vows. In this vein, she criticized not only the European Catholics but also the Kongo rulers. She charged that they were fighting their wars for personal gain and not for the public good. Not one of them was fit to be king.

Beatriz burned not only the old fetishes but also the Christian cross. She believed in direct communication with God and with the other world, as she had practiced as an *nganga marinda*, and she had no need of any special objects of worship, including the cross.

In Beatriz's time, the oral traditions in the kingdom revered Afonso as the bringer of Christianity to Kongo. So Beatriz's claim that Christ had been born in São Salvador (where Afonso had reigned and built the first churches) and baptized in Nsundi (where Afonso had been governor) simply conformed to the oral traditions already in place.

In these ways, Beatriz invented an ideology that took the best of both worlds and appealed to many Esikongo—especially the peasants. Unfortunately, she found herself in a position that could not be tolerated by either the Capuchin missionaries or the Kongo ruling class.

The Old Kingdom Dies

Beatriz was born around 1686 and possessed by Saint Anthony in 1704. Why did she appear when she did? Why not earlier in Kongo's history, or later?

Beatriz's story is similar to that of Joan of Arc—a fifteenth-century French peasant whose religious visions and courage enabled her to lead an army to victory. She too was burned at the stake as a heretic. In southeast Africa, in the mid-nineteenth century, a young Xhosa (KOH suh) maiden named Nonquase also had deeply religious visions. Unfortunately her visions led her people to commit suicide by killing off most of their cattle, their main source of food. In each of these cases, a spiritual leader arose when radically different cultures came into conflict and a nation had been in turmoil for a long period.

So it was in Kongo. At first, and for a whole century after Afonso's death in 1543, the kingdom experienced a period of great expansion. This growth was fueled partly by the slave trade, but mostly by the cloth trade with the colony of Angola, farther to the south. In fact, by 1610, Kongo was exporting 100,000 m (110,000 yd) of cloth a year to Angola—an extraordinary amount for the time.

There were minor setbacks to this expansion. In 1568, for example, the kingdom was invaded by the ferocious Imbangala—a warrior people from the east who were known to be cannibals. With Portuguese help, they were eventually driven back.

The critical event that led to the kingdom's ruin occurred in the 1630s, when the large and powerful province of Soyo broke away from Kongo. Soyo harbored rival branches of the royal *kanda*, with members who were candidates for the throne. On October 29, 1665, the Portuguese fought Kongo in an insignificant battle over a small territory called Mbwila. Yet the battle proved to be the turning point in Kongo's history. During the fray the reigning king was killed. With no designated successor to the throne, the country erupted into civil war as the royal rivals fought bitterly over the throne.

> In Kongo, there had never been strict provisions for the succession to the throne. It was not an ancestral position, but one for which members of the royal family competed. Often, after a king died, war broke out between rival claimants until one or other of them won. The fighting provided the Esikongo leaders with many war captives, who later were sold as slaves to the Europeans.

 Severe drought possibly drove them to invade the kingdom.

In the process, the old city of Mbanza Kongo, which had been renamed São Salvador, was destroyed and abandoned. Without a capital, the rival branches of the royal family seized various provinces and waged war continually over who would repopulate and control the capital. The civil war provided hundreds of thousands of captives, who were sold into slavery.

Life in the kingdom became impossible. Peasants could not grow their crops or continue their daily lives. They were in constant danger, either from cross-fire or from slavers. Thousands abandoned their villages and took refuge from the endless wars in far-off mountain regions. The entire system of trade, tribute, and power was upset. By 1700 a generation of Esikongo had grown up never knowing a period of peace.

It is not so surprising, then, that when Beatriz arose as a powerful leader, she found many followers. It is also not surprising that she was seen as a major threat, not only to the Catholic establishment but also to the political hierarchy of the king- dom. When she pro- claimed herself Kongo's spiritual leader, for exam- ple, she immediately antago- nized the *kitome* chiefs, who saw themselves as the nation's spiritual leaders. When Beatriz crowned Pedro Constantinho da Silva as king, she removed that authority from oth- ers who claimed that office. Although Beatriz's very ashes were burned so that no

"holy relics" might remain, the Antonian movement did not die out immediately. Like a lingering flame, there was hope that the kingdom might revive. But slavery, greed, and war had done their damage.

By the end of the eighteenth cen- tury, São Salvador was a pitiful collection of huts. In the 1950s, a British traveler named Clement Egerton visited the site and interviewed a 70- year-old man who claimed to be Dom Pedro VII, last king of the Kongo.

The old man lived in a modest house. His walls were hung with pictures of Portuguese royalty. He received a small stipend from the Portuguese authorities and grew a little coffee and rice.

Egerton was shown the royal regalia. There was "a royal robe trimmed with white fur, which looked more like rabbit than ermine, and a silver crown, a scepter, and miscellaneous utensils."

In 1955 the old man died. He was the last descen- dent of the Kongo kings.

◄ In 1914 the British missionary John Weeks photographed Mbembe, King Pedro VI of Kongo. The robes and the silver scepter were a present from the king of Portugal in 1888. They were state property and passed from the king to his successor. When Clement Egerton visited São Salvador in the 1950s, he saw the last remaining relics of the royal regalia.

Ndongo—From Ngola to Angola

Njinga: The Warrior Queen

I am an old woman now, with few years to live. As we sit here, Father Giovanni, I will tell you my stories, and you will write them down. Thus may future generations know the story of Queen Njinga (JIHN guh)!

I have suffered much. I fought for my power. But in my youth, I watched while my brother Mbandi tottered on the throne. What right had this cowardly weakling to become king? By mere virtue of being our father's son, did he seize the throne and the title of Ngola. But there was no merit to him.

Ah, what sorrow did Ngola Mbandi cause me! First he took my first-born son and sent him to the Kingdom of Heaven—murdered, so that he should never oppose my brother. Then he took the throne but could not lead his people. Instead we Mbundu have been persecuted, killed, our lands plundered, our people captured into slavery. I myself, dear Father, lost my own husband in battle.

And you, Father, soon will administer the last rites to this poor body. And what will you write of me, Njinga? Will you write of my great battles, as I led my people, fearlessly, my arrows speeding true and fast? Will you write that my banners flew high and proud and that Portuguese soldiers quivered before them?

Perhaps, Father Giovanni, you will write of the evil the Portuguese have done to our lands. In my youth I had hope. Surely, I believed, there must be some good in these men who came from afar. But each new governor proved worse than the last. Greedy are they, Father Giovanni. Greedy, proud, and stupid, for they say they come in peace, yet do they wage unceasing war.

I learned patience, Father Giovanni. All around me there was nothing but suffering. I vowed that one day I would avenge my brother for the death of my son. And I would avenge the Portuguese for the death of my country.

Ah, those Portuguese are cunning jackals! What promises they made us! I recall Louis Mendes de Vasconcellos, that new governor of Luanda. What pledges of friendship he made, and of peaceful trade! We should become Christians, he said. He showed us royal decrees sent by his king, ordering his people to help us, the people of Mbundu. What need have we, who have lived for so long in these realms, of outside help? Perhaps in your wisdom, Father Giovanni, you have an answer to this question.

What sweet words Vasconcellos used! But we watched from afar and awaited the treachery we knew would come.

Vasconcellos demanded tribute from my brother Ngola Mbandi, king of Ndongo. As though Ndongo were a vassal state of the Portuguese! We refused, and his revenge was swift, for he destroyed our capital at Kabasa by fire. We fled before him, taking hostages whom we hid on an island in the river. Vasconcellos's rage knew no bounds. Oh, Father Giovanni, nothing can measure our grief when we learned that he had executed our Mbundu chieftains.

What were we now but a land of refuges with a king who hid himself in fear on an island? Now we faced also the Imbangala—those warriors from the east. They joined the Portuguese and hounded us like dogs in the bush. They captured our people and sold them to the *pombeiros*—those cursed men of mixed blood, who have made it their work to sell our people to their masters.

Truly, Father Giovanni, our great kingdom lay in ruins. Our people were starving, and our children had never known peace. My brother, the king, dared not even leave his island refuge! How we yearned for a truce! But now we heard that a new governor had arrived in Luanda. Word filtered back to us that this man, named Jaoa Correia de Souza, wished to sign a peace treaty. He had lost too many men to our arrows and to sickness. He had lost too much trade.

You may think me proud and stubborn, Father Giovanni. But it was at this time in my life that I decided to take matters into my own hands. Perhaps I could persuade this de Souza to help us rid our land of the Imbangala. Thus, I went to Luanda as Ngola Mbandi's ambassador. I made the journey with a hard heart and a strong will. I would not give in to these usurpers! The treaty should be fair and of benefit to both sides, or I would not sign it.

Thus did I come face to face with this Correia de Souza, in the great rooms of his mansion in Luanda. But I was cunning, Father Giovanni. Do you think I wished to appear as some flighty maiden, to beg on her knees before this

arrogant stranger? No! I came with my women, my guard of honor. And when we entered the reception room, my women went forward first, splendidly clad, as a phalanx fit to greet a governor and to guard an ambassador.

The room was filled with people whom the governor had commanded to attend, and great was their astonishment when they beheld me! Oh, Father Giovanni, this was a proud moment! I saw soldiers with gleaming helmets, and ladies stiff with skirts and jewels. I saw gentlemen, powdered and ruffed, with plumed hats and great swords. I saw many of your priests, darkly clad against the richness of the scene.

There sat de Souza, in a great carved chair on a raised dais. For me there was but a carpet, strewn with cushions. Did they think that I, Njinga, would deign

In 1622, Njinga met with the Portuguese governor, Joao Correia de Souza, in Luanda.

to sit on the floor while this arrogant foreigner looked down upon me from his throne? Never! I gave no hint of my thoughts but clapped my hands for my maid. She understood at once and knelt before me on all fours. I sat upon her back, and a better throne I have never had!

Father Giovanni, I smile today when I recall that scene. How shocked were the guests! What murmurs and whispers fled about the great hall! But de Souza was a man of mettle. He too showed not by a muscle his true feelings but made me welcome in the name of his sovereign, King Felipe IV of Portugal.

Now do you write this down, Father Giovanni, for this is how I wish to be remembered.

I allowed the governor to speak first. He told of his regret for events of the past, of the bloodshed, death, and ill will that had so long plagued our nations. I waited. "We wish to live in peace with the Mbundu," he said. "We wish to trade so that both nations may benefit. And we wish to bring you the word of our Savior, Jesus Christ, so that your people may enter the Kingdom of Heaven."

I had no interest in these words, for we had heard them before. Patiently, I waited for the conditions of the treaty.

"If your king, Ngola Mbandi, will release those soldiers and traders he now holds hostage, I offer him a treaty of friendship."

I would not make things easy for Governor Correia de Souza. "We too yearn to see our people returned and unharmed," I replied. "You have taken our brothers and sisters, our fathers and uncles. May we not expect their return, also?"

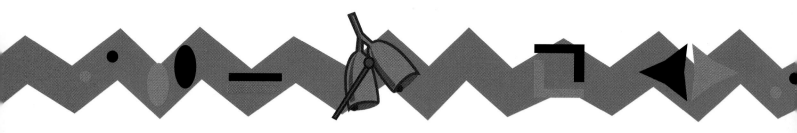

Again, the guests rustled and whispered. Did I dare oppose their governor? I did!

"If you meet our conditions," the governor continued, "I am prepared to accept the right of Ndongo to exist as an independent kingdom, with Ngola Mbandi on the throne."

My heart quivered in anger, but still I showed nothing. What were these foolish words? Was Ndongo not already an independent kingdom, ruled by our kings for centuries past! But de Souza had said he would accept my brother as king. This was joyful news, for until then the Portuguese had claimed their puppet, that traitor Ngola Hari, as the king of Ndongo and would accept no other.

Now I asked the governor what returns he required in exchange for these concessions. The audience hushed, eager to hear his words.

"If Ndongo is to be recognized as a kingdom," he smiled, "we will expect an annual tribute, to be discussed at a later date."

Scorn filled my being. "Ngola Mbandi has no need to pay tribute!" I replied. "If the governor wishes to live in peace, he has only to withdraw his troops from our lands. You have destroyed Ndongo and caused our people to suffer great hunger and sorrow. But we are not conquered. Tribute, O governor, can be demanded only from a conquered people!"

I had my strength, Father Giovanni. I knew I must not for a moment show weakness or guile. And in de Souza's eyes I saw that he recognized me as an equal. Now we began the work of building the treaty, piece by piece, as one builds a house. And after many hours we came to agree. I promised that we would return the Portuguese hostages. We would also

gather up those fugitive slaves who had sought refuge in our lands and deliver them to the governor. On his part, he would withdraw his people from our towns, and he would help us to expel the Imbangala from Ndongo.

These were but the details, Father Giovanni. But the true glory came at the moment when we signed the treaty, for we signed not as conqueror and vassal, but as equals, as brothers in peace, as representatives of two independent nations. Of this, Father Giovanni, I am most proud.

As I prepare to join my ancestors, Father Giovanni, I am at peace. I have given my life for my people. I have taken another name, Dona Anna de Souza, that I might join your faith. When I am gone, I beg you to clothe me in your Capuchin habit, that my people may see me in the true faith. And I ask you to bury me in my royal robes, and to lay my bow and arrow upon my breast. And may these tales that I have related to you forever guard the true spirit of Anna de Souza, Queen Njinga of Ndongo and Matamba.

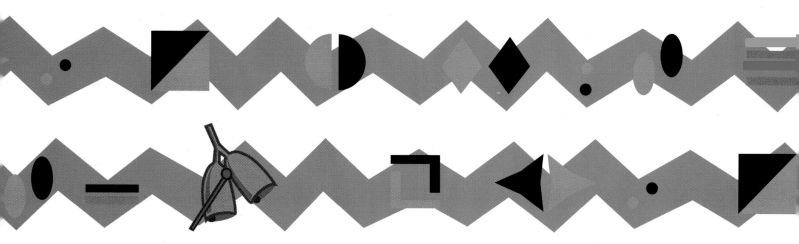

Father Giovanni Antonio Cavazzi heard Njinga's stories from the queen herself and made many drawings and paintings recording her life. He depicted himself here with African chapel boys.

Fact and Fiction

Njinga of Ndongo—or Queen Njinga of Matamba, as she later came to be known—has gone down in history as a quite remarkable woman. However, there is much controversy surrounding her story.

To begin with, the historic meeting with Correia de Souza was never actually recorded at the time! The story—and most of the rest of Njinga's colorful life history—was first written down in 1658 by the Capuchin missionary Giovanni Antonio Gaeta da Napoli. In 1687, Giovanni Antonio Cavazzi published his version of Njinga's story, but there were many other eyewitness reports written during her lifetime.

Father Giovanni attended Njinga during her final years, when she had become a devout Catholic, and

Governor Vasconcellos had good intentions when he arrived in Luanda in the early 1600s. He denounced the traders and conquistadores who had ruined the land. But after only four years in Luanda, he had become a very rich man through the slave trade. He completely altered his views about Angola: "It is only through severity and fear that we can hold our own against these indomitable heathens." These were his words of advice to his successor, Governor Correia de Souza.

administered the last rites to her when she lay dying. He took the information for his chronicles from Njinga herself. She undoubtedly wished to die a heroine and probably tailored her story to her own advantage.

Njinga may have done this because she had alienated the Mbundu people, whom she claimed as her followers. First, they expressly forbade women to hold positions of power. Although some supported her as a candidate to the throne by descent, they automatically disqualified her because she was a woman. Second, there were those who questioned her lineage. They said that she was descended from a different mother than Ngola Mbandi, and could therefore not be considered kin at all. Others said that her father was a slave at the royal court, a man with no lineage to speak of. It was also not known whether Njinga was really Ngola Mbandi's "ambassador." It is quite possible that she simply took this role upon herself, turning it to her best advantage.

Njinga signed the treaty with Correia de Souza in 1622. She remained at Luanda for several months, receiving instruction from the Jesuit priests in preparation for

▲ Njinga was baptized in 1622. She used the Catholic name of Dona Anna de Souza, in honor of the governor.

her baptism. For Njinga knew that if she was to get anywhere with the Portuguese, she would have to accept their faith, even if only in name. The Portuguese hoped that Njinga herself would help spread Catholicism in Ndongo.

The baptism was a grand ceremony attended by all of Luanda society. In honor of Governor de Souza, Njinga renamed herself Dona Anna de Souza.

Immediately afterwards, she departed for the island camp of the king, Ngola Mbandi.

For the next 40 years Njinga played a very important role in the politics of Angola. In Portugal, Njinga is still regularly featured in school textbooks. And in Brazil, popular plays called *congoadas* (con goh AH duhz) feature Queen Njinga exchanging embassies with the king of Kongo.

After the Treaty

The Portuguese knew they had to gain control over Angola's interior if they were to profit from trade. They were also the allies of the puppet king, Angola Hari, who had agreed to become their vassal. The war waged from 1624 to 1655 was over who would rule Ndongo: the Portuguese, with Ngola Hari on the throne; Njinga's half-brother Ngola Mbandi; or Njinga herself.

Angola was the name the Portuguese originally used for the territory of Ndongo. This was a corruption of the Mbundu word *ngola* which was probably a royal title or the name of an iron emblem of authority.

◄ Photographed in 1975, this Mbundu chief wears a headdress similar to those depicted by Cavazzi in 1687, which were worn by the kings and queens of Angola and Matamba.

In keeping with the terms of the treaty, Ngola Mbandi released his Portuguese hostages. But his spies reported that the Portuguese were not withdrawing. Instead they were fortifying their strongholds in Ndongo. Eventually, Mbandi learned that Governor de Souza had been recalled to Lisbon. The new governor ignored the peace treaty.

At this point, Njinga sought the help of Kaza, leader of a group of Imbangala. These people were mercenary warriors who hired themselves out to anyone who would pay them. Apparently Kaza accepted Njinga's authority, for he agreed to form an alliance with her. Meanwhile, Njinga's half brother Ngola Mbandi committed suicide. It is said that Njinga murdered his young son, who would have been the next king.

Njinga's alliance grew to include several Mbundu chieftains. They closed off all trade routes and confined the Portuguese to the coast. This was the final straw. The Portuguese called for aid from Lisbon, and when it came, they declared all-out war against Njinga.

The aging queen used clever tactics to keep her army intact. She was driven ever farther east, away from the grassy plains of Ndongo. But she did not give up. Instead, she led her people on a long and dreadful march even farther east, to the ancient kingdom of Matamba. Here, Njinga captured the reigning queen, had her branded as a slave, and took the throne of Matamba herself.

For the next ten years, Queen Njinga held fast in Matamba. With Kaza and

his Imbangala people among her soldiers, she had to tolerate their cannibal rites. She deliberately kept all her movements secret and often allowed false rumors of her actions to reach the Portuguese. When Kaza abandoned Njinga in 1628, she lacked manpower, but outdid the Portuguese in cunning.

In 1639, the new governor of Luanda tried to make peace with Njinga. He sent ambassadors, a priest, and a nobleman fluent in the Mbundu language. But they returned empty-handed.

Meanwhile, the Dutch—who were as thirsty for trade as the Portuguese—had arrived near the Zaire River and were trading with the kingdom of Kongo. The Protestant Dutch and the Catholic Portuguese were dire enemies. They had clashed in Europe, in Brazil, on the west coast of Africa, and in the Far East. It was to be no different in Ndongo.

In 1641, Dutch ships came south and anchored near Luanda. They had vastly superior forces and gun power to the Portuguese, who sensibly withdrew to their farms inland, leaving the Dutch to occupy Luanda.

◀ This sculpture from central Angola is an effigy of a nineteenth-century king. The upturned hairstyle and huge hands and feet reflect the king's power and strength.

There followed a series of tremendous wars. In 1647–1648, Njinga's army besieged Massangano, the Portuguese stronghold. Had the city fallen, Njinga would have conquered Portuguese Angola. But the city held. Meanwhile, in Lisbon, King Joao IV had decided to regain Angola at all costs. In May 1648, a well-equipped armada led by Salvador de Saa set sail from Rio de Janeiro in Brazil, arriving in Luanda a few weeks later. By this time, the Dutch had become less interested in Angola and more interested in regions farther south on the continent. To everyone's surprise, they surrendered to de Saa without a fight and departed.

Once again, the Portuguese were determined to gain control of Angola, and of Kongo to the north, where trade relations had also deteriorated. Njinga's alliance of African chiefs had begun to crumble, and it was now to her advantage to negotiate again with the Portuguese.

In fact, both sides recognized a stalemate, and a peace treaty was signed in 1656. This time, the Mbundu territory was clearly defined. The Matamba kingdom, which Njinga occupied, was bound by the Lukala River on the west, the Kwango on the east, the Kwanza on the south, and the kingdom of Kongo to the north. Njinga opened Matamba to the slave traders but retained a monopoly over slave exports. She agreed to send an annual tribute of slaves to Luanda. Both sides agreed to get rid of the troublesome Imbangala.

During a battle before the peace, one of Njinga's warriors had found a crucifix. Njinga regarded this as a sign that she must renew her Christian faith. Consultation with a captured Catholic priest and with her own spirit mediums encouraged her reconversion. She agreed to renounce the Imbangala practices of cannibalism and human sacrifice that she had taken up while using their warriors. She built several churches in Matamba and, at the age of 75, even married one of her followers.

Queen Njinga of Matamba will always be an enigmatic figure. She was a woman of extraordinary intelligence, courage, and skill. Yet she was also cruel, violent, and cunning. She died in 1663, aged 81, attended by the good Father Antonio Giovanni Cavazzi.

Epilogue

COFFEE

SUGAR CANE

The Portuguese colony of Angola eventually grew to include Kongo, Ndongo, and a number of lesser states. Despite war, deadly tropical diseases, and all the discomforts of life below the equator, the Portuguese persisted in Kongo and Ndongo into the late twentieth century.

But the Portuguese did not take control easily. Their efforts spanned several centuries, and there was strong resistance from different sections of the African population. King Afonso, Beatriz Kimpa Vita, Queen Njinga—these are the heroes and heroines of a resistance movement that persists in Angola to the present day.

In Kongo the authority of the kings declined as the demand for slaves increased. Mbanza Kongo, the capital, had been the main center of trade and the traditional residence of the king for centuries. But as the Portuguese settled along the coast, they developed new trade routes into the interior, bypassing the capital and thus the king's control.

These routes brought slaves and other goods to the important province of Soyo at the mouth of the Zaire River, which then surpassed Mbanza Kongo as a slave trading center. Soyo had always been a fairly independent province that appointed its own rulers and was influential in electing new kings. The province

TOBACCO

profited so greatly from the slave trade that it was no longer economically tied to Mbanza Kongo.

When the Dutch arrived on the Kongo coast in the seventeenth century, the competition for slaves increased. In the early eighteenth century, the English became major slave traders. The civil wars in Kongo at this time provided traders with thousands of captives, who were exported through ports just north of the Zaire River along the Loanga coast. In fact, at least a fifth of all Africans sent to the Americas came from Kongo and traveled through these ports.

By the end of the eighteenth century, the French had become major exporters of African slaves. In fact, about half of the population of the then French colony of Haiti came from Kongo. They played an important role in the Haitian revolution of 1791, when slaves overthrew the French government of the island. One of

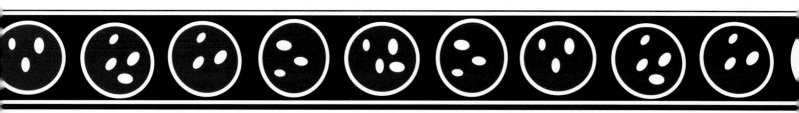

their revolutionary leaders, named Macaya, claimed that he had served the king of Kongo.

Kongo was eventually reunited in the eighteenth century under Dom Pedro IV. But civil wars had brought about drastic changes, and the new "kingdom" was more of an old memory than an actual fact.

The same was true of Ndongo. With the growth of the slave trade, the island of São Tomé had developed into the main export center of slaves to the Portuguese colony of Brazil. Eventually, the São Tomé traders set up another major export center at Luanda. From there they purchased slaves from the king, or *ngola* of Ndongo. This increased his power enormously; he was able to expand his kingdom westward, toward the coast, just as the Portuguese were attempting to penetrate the interior. By the mid-eighteenth century,

◀ These slaves wait to be placed on board a ship to Brazil. They are guarded by an African trader. Historians calculate that about 20 percent of slaves in North America and 60 percent of the slaves on Haiti originally came from Angola.

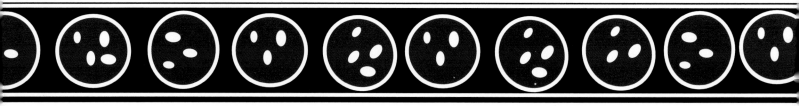

Luanda was exporting over 10,000 slaves a year, more than any other place on the African coast.

With the slave trade came missionaries. Many were heavily involved in the slave trade, and their hypocrisy was well noted by the African people. First came the Portuguese Catholics and then the Dutch Protestants and later came Baptists, Anglicans, Methodists, and representatives of other religions. All of them tried to influence the Angolans by putting down their native belief systems. Amazingly enough, the old beliefs survived and are still practiced by about half of the 10 million people living in the region today.

OLD LUANDA AND NEW LUANDA

Luanda grew from a small town in the fifteenth century (as shown above) to a large city in the twentieth century. ▶

The slave trade declined during the 1800s, but its impact on African economic development was far-reaching. In exchange for captives, traders had imported guns, Indian cottons, and cheap Brazilian rum. No investment was made in African crafts and industry. Instead, the Portuguese developed coffee and cocoa plantations alongside their sugar cane and tobacco farms in the central highlands in Angola. In the late 1920s the Portuguese government decided to improve the region's economy. Soon afterwards, thousands of Portuguese immigrants flooded into Angola to set up businesses or farms. New industries, such as fishing and mining for diamonds and iron ore, were developed. Railways and roads were built. Luanda became a major seaport. Mbanza Kongo and Soyo became important centers of oil production.

Even today, however, Angola's economy is still based in agriculture. Seventy-five percent of its people are farmers or herders, living in rural areas. The Mbundu and the Bakongo are still among the largest ethnic groups there

A woman dries fish for export from Luanda. ▶

and still speak their Bantu languages. Europeans, educated Africans, and mestizos—people of mixed blood—speak Portuguese.

By the 1950s the Angolans had been under Portuguese authority for almost 500 years. The coffee industry had taken over large tracts of native farmland, and Portuguese immigrants crowded Angolan towns. The government had neglected to educate the Angolan people, who were tired of their inferior position in their own country. At this time, many other African nations were seeking and

▲ Young Angolan girls wearing beaded headdresses and brightly colored skirts perform a traditional dance.

winning their independence from the colonial powers. Angola would not be left out, although its struggle would take some time.

In 1956 the Popular Movement for the Liberation of Angola (MPLA) was formed. In 1961, northern rebels formed the Front for the Liberation of Angola (FNLA) and sparked a revolt that spread throughout the nation. The FNLA was based on a faction of the Kongo royal *kanda*. Four years later, southern rebels formed the National Union for Total Independence of Angola (UNITA). To quell the fighting and regain control over its colony, Portugal mobilized an army of 60,000 soldiers. For the next 13 years, Angola was consumed by civil war as rival groups battled for power.

In 1975, Portugal withdrew from Angola and its other colonies in Africa, leaving the nation open to exploitation

This young Mbundu man is a soldier for the MPLA. He carries a Soviet gun. ▶

Today the people of Angola have no voice in their government. The Popular Movement for the Liberation of Angola is the only political party in the country. Much like the old kings of Kongo and Ndongo, the party leader serves as the nation's president, head of state, and commander in chief of the armed forces.

by other powers, each with its own goals. Zaire supported the FNLA. South Africa supported UNITA. And the Communist nations of Cuba and the former Soviet Union supported the MPLA. France, Britain, and the United States all became involved in support of one group or another.

Just as in Kongo during the seventeenth century, and for much the same reasons, the civil war continued with unabated fury. The war broke down transportation systems and disrupted food production. Most Europeans fled the country. Business, agriculture, fish-ing, mining—all came to a virtual standstill. After several attempted cease-fires, an election was held in 1992. The MPLA won, but rival groups would not accept the results, and fighting broke out again. By this time, some 2 million Angolans—about a fifth of the total population—were refugees, totally dependent on outside aid from various organizations for food and shelter.

In 1994 a new truce was signed. This time, perhaps, it will hold, allowing Angola finally to renew its ties to the past and to build toward a peaceful future.

Pronunciation Key

Some words in this book may be new to you or difficult to pronounce. Those words have been spelled phonetically in parentheses. The syllable that receives stress in a word is shown in small capital letters. The following pronunciation key shows how letters are used to show different sounds.

a	after	(AF tur)	oh	flow	(floh)	ch	chicken	(CHIHK un)
ah	father	(FAH thur)	oi	boy	(boi)	g	game	(gaym)
ai	care	(kair)	oo	rule	(rool)	ing	coming	(KUM ing)
aw	dog	(dawg)	or	horse	(hors)	j	job	(jahb)
ay	paper	(PAY pur)	ou	cow	(kou)	k	came	(kaym)
			yoo	few	(fyoo)	ng	long	(lawng)
e	letter	(LET ur)	u	taken	(TAY kun)	s	city	(SIH tee)
ee	eat	(eet)		matter	(MAT ur)	sh	ship	(shihp)
			uh	ago	(uh goh)	th	thin	(thihn)
ih	trip	(trihp)				thh	feather	(FETHH ur)
eye	idea	(eye DEE uh)				y	yard	(yahrd)
y	hide	(hyd)				z	size	(syz)
ye	lie	(lye)				zh	division	(duh VIHZH un)

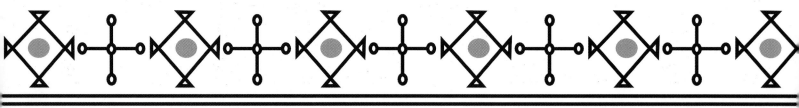

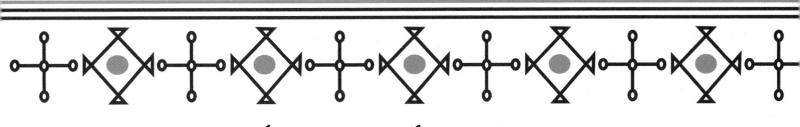

For Further Reading

(* = recommended for younger readers)

Balandier, Georges. *Daily Life in the Kingdom of Kongo*. New York: Pantheon Books, 1968.

Boyd, Herb. *African History for Beginners*. New York: Writers and Readers Publishing, 1991.*

Davidson, Basil. *Africa in History*. New York: Macmillan, 1991.

———. *African Kingdoms*. New York: Time-Life Books, 1966.

———. *A Guide to African History*. New York: Doubleday, Zenith Books, 1965.

———. *The Lost Cities of Africa*. Boston: Little, Brown 1970.

DeGraft-Johnson, J. C. *African Glory*. New York: Walker, 1954.

Delgado, Ralph. *Historia de Angola* (A History of Angola). 2 vols. Lisbon: Edicao de Banco de Angola.

Dobler, Lavinia. *Great Kingdoms of the African Past*. New York: Doubleday, Zenith Books, 1965.*

Harris, Joseph E. *African Kingdoms and Their History*. New York: New American Library, 1987.

Hilton, Anne. *The Kingdom of Kongo*. New York: Oxford University Press, 1985.

Ki-Zerbo, Joseph. *Die Geschichte Schwarz-Afrikas* (The History of Black Africa). Wuppertal: Peter Hammer, 1979.

Kwamena-Poh, Michael. *African History in Maps*. London: Longman, 1982.

McEvedy, Collin. *The Penguin Atlas of African History*. London: Penguin Books, 1980.*

Miller, Joseph. "Nzinga of Matamba in a New Perspective." *Journal of African History* 16. 2 (1975): 202–16.

Murray, Jocelyn. *Cultural Atlas of Africa*. New York: Facts on File, 1989.*

Oliver, Ronald. *The African Experience*. New York: HarperCollins, 1991.

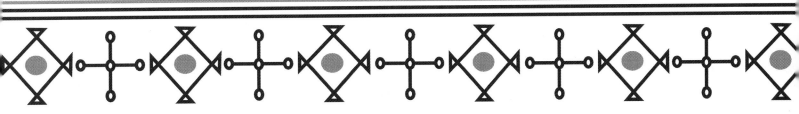

———. *The Dawn of African History*. London: Oxford University Press, 1968.

Oliver, Roland, and J. D. Fage. *A Short History of Africa*. 6th ed. London: Penguin Books, 1988.

Pigafetta, Filippo. *A Report of the Kingdom of Kongo*. London: John Murray, 1881. Reprint. London: Frank Cass, 1970.

Polatnick, Florence, and B. Saletan. *Shapers of Africa*. New York: J. Messner, 1969.

Schachtzabel, Alfred. *Im Hochland von Angola* (In the Highlands of Angola). Deutsche Buchwerkstatten, 1923.

Scholefield, A. *The Dark Kingdoms*. New York: William Morrow, 1975.

Stacey, Tom. *Peoples of the Earth*. Tom Stacey and Europa Verlag, 1972.*

Thornton, John K. *The Kingdom of Kongo: Civil War and Transition, 1641–1718*. Madison: University of Wisconsin Press, 1983.

Weeks, John H. *Among the Primitive Bakongo*. London: Seely, Service, 1914.

Wheeler, Douglas L., and R. Pelissier. *Angola*. London: Pall Mall Press,

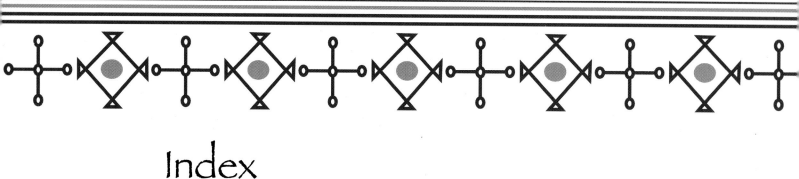

Index

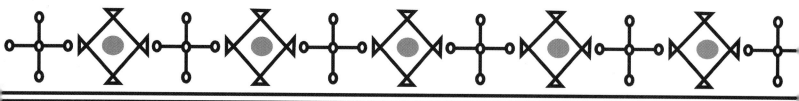